SUMMER 62

MADEMOISELLE
COCO CHANEL SUMMER 62

PHOTOGRAPHS DOUGLAS KIRKLAND

TEXT KARL LAGERFELD

STEIDL

" Quand le présent dont je suis revêtue

   Aura trahi,…

   Vous referez mon nom et mon image."

                                    Catherine Pozzi

" In this alone we suffer:

   Cut off from hope, we live on in desire."

                                    Dante: Inferno

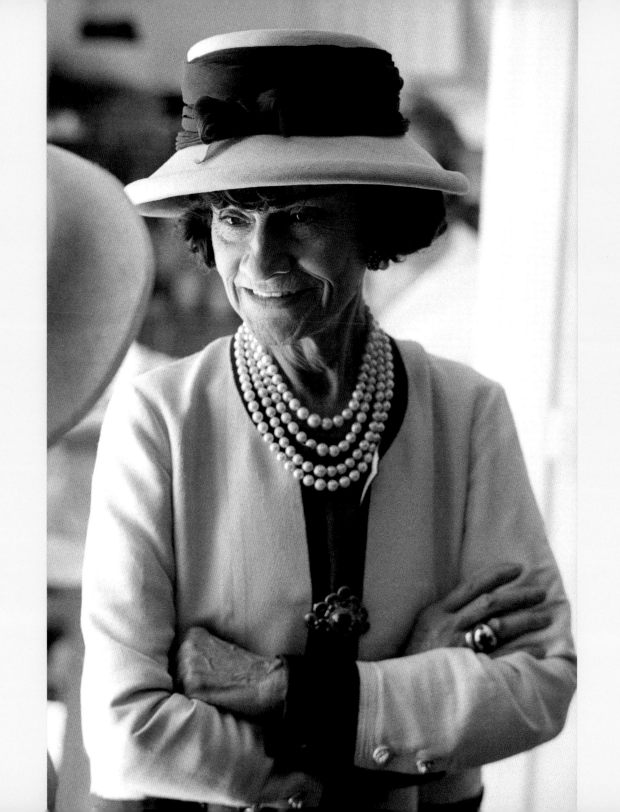

SUMMER 62

Visually Douglas Kirkland investigates a past unknown to us, beyond our reach without him. Things gone forever return in the most authentic way possible through his recollection of these "moments privilegiés". We vaguely know the history of Chanel, but suddenly it's all alive, we feel connected with something that seemed entirely remote before. We witness the vanished power of an unusual reign in the world of fashion. Reality has melted and diluted, but those images have not faded.

We can see them as a halo and a suggestion of short moments of happiness (or we want to believe they had been happy ones) during that summer, late but not too late towards the end of her life.

There is a deep and intimate charm in Douglas Kirkland's photos of "Mademoiselle". He removed from her image all its evils and the

bitchy side popular imagination has attached to her persona. It's a reduction of all clichés concerning Coco Chanel to immediate appreciation, sympathy and nearly cheerfulness.
Seen by Douglas Kirkland, she is no longer an older woman. Famous people are not judged on how they are but on what they are.
Time was running out, but as T.S. Eliot says in the poem "If Time and Space as Sages Say":

"To live a century?
The butterfly that lives a day
Has lived eternity."

She still had nearly 9 years to go.
Looking at the camera of this young and handsome American she

seems to say: Whatever you gave me, and if it was only a smile, you cannot take back. I can keep it like a treasure forever.

Summer 62 was, in a way, her last summer as the queen of fashion. Jeans and miniskirts were on their way to invade the world. Hating them and letting people know publicly how much she loathed the fashions to come she put herself instantly in the position of the has-been oracle of style and fashion.

The years to come were clouded for her by gloom and bitterness. They were also the years of respect, hommage (a word the French love) and all those evident signs which tell you your time is over. The word "vintage" was not yet invented. Suddenly nobody was interested in the past. Childish futurism (seen what the world became finally) was the next step in fashion.

The name of Chanel could only come back without her in a new corporate world of fashion the way we know it today. Her name as a brand was the first to be reborn. Many others followed.

Here suddenly, during the short weeks of July 1962, a young all-American boy brought back her once so irresistible black-sun smile. She never made a big effort for women but this young man was a perfect target to test for the last time her once famous powers of seduction. There are hardly any photos of her – even when young – with such a winning smile, with such a lightness in her expression. When working she is another person, looking more serious than the job requires. There is the famous fitting of the armhole, but there are also a few sweet moments of complicity with some of the models, but in a charming, condescending way – nothing to do with the spontaneity of her ageless smile when she looks at Kirkland's camera.

She had had time to tell the world that she had invented it all, that she was the modern woman who suddenly hated modernity. All the other designers, some of them as influencial as she was in the first 40 years of the 20th century, were suddenly forgotten. They were men and women with none of Coco's charm and beauty.

Images left behind are finally stronger than truth and facts. Through Douglas Kirkland's images we can imagine what the famous Coco had been all about before she became the formidable Chanel, the feminine version of the statue of the Commendatore in Mozart's opera "Don Giovanni", wearing the uniform she invented like an invincible armour...

Karl Lagerfeld

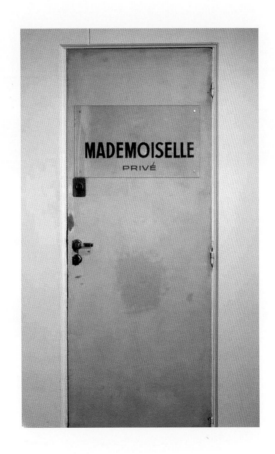

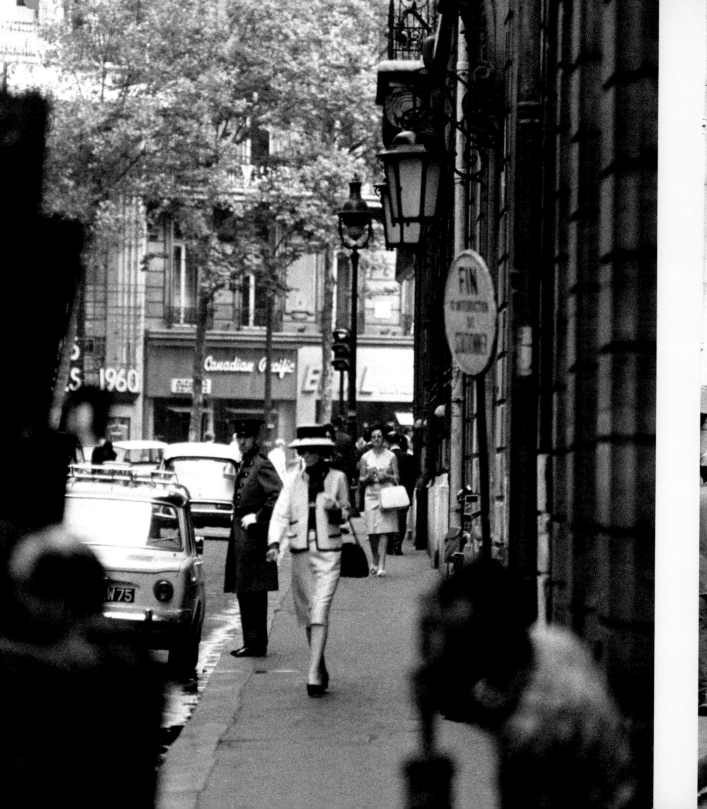
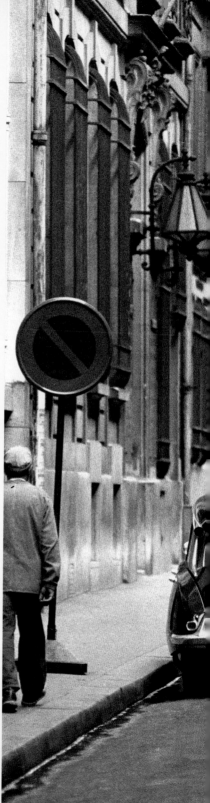

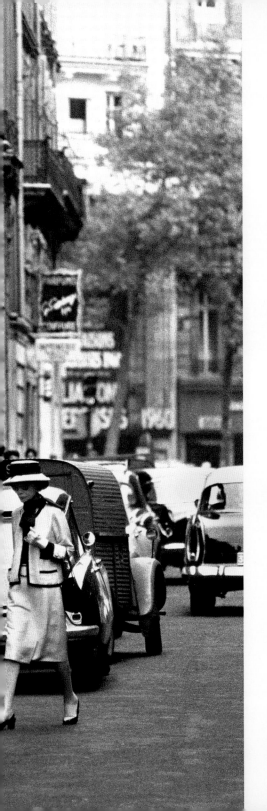
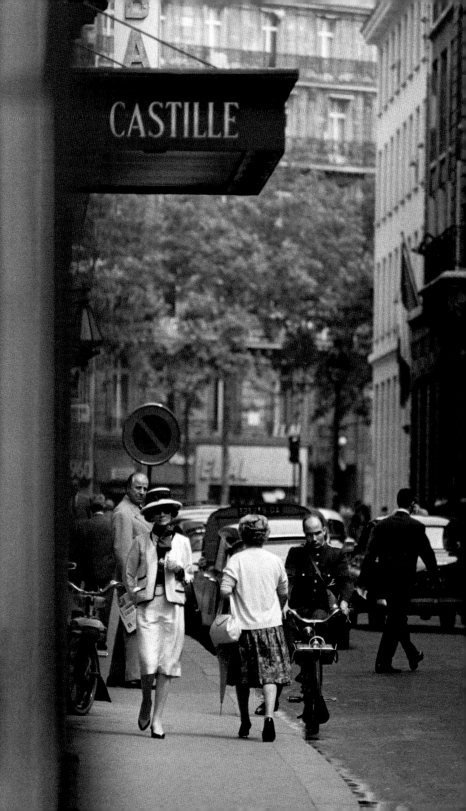

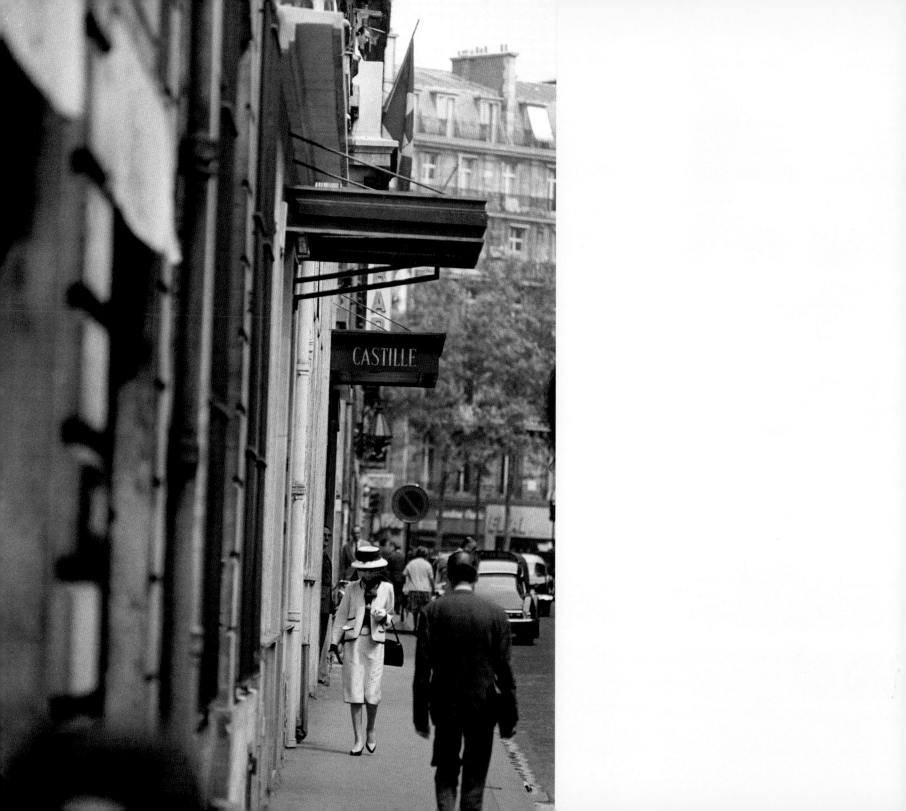

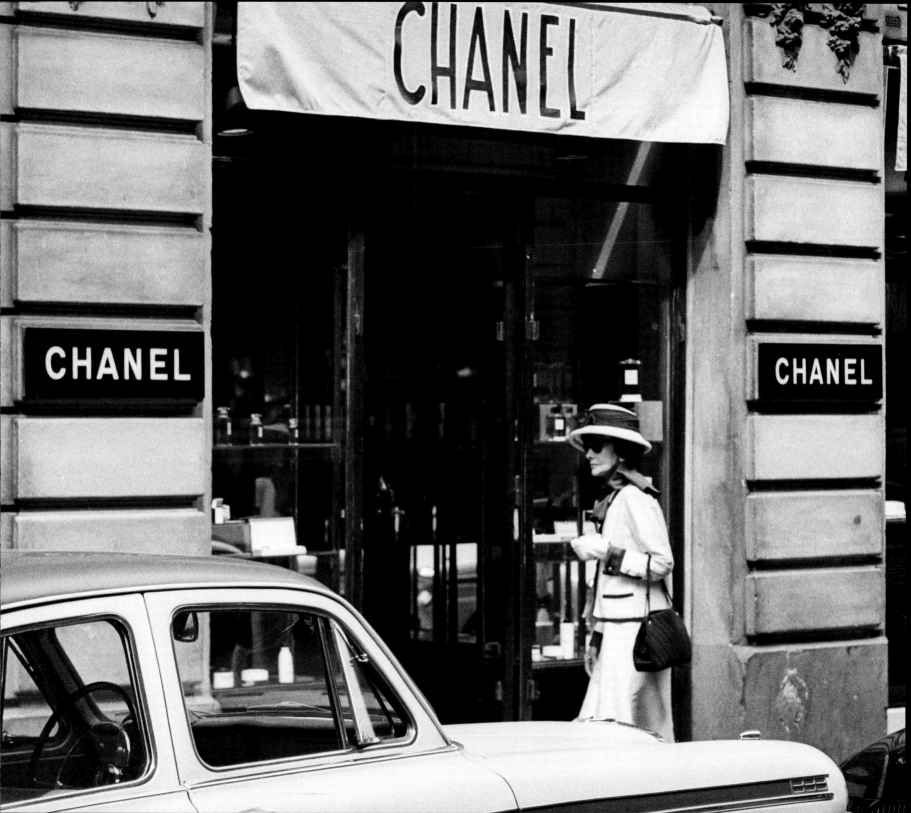

THE MYTHIC STAIRCASE

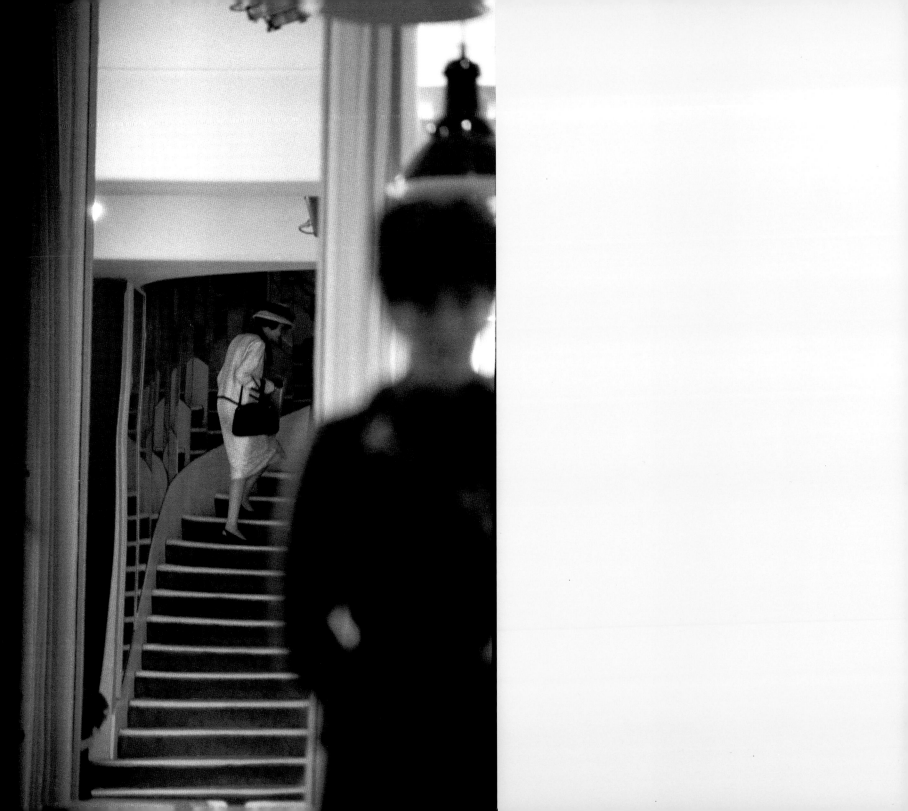

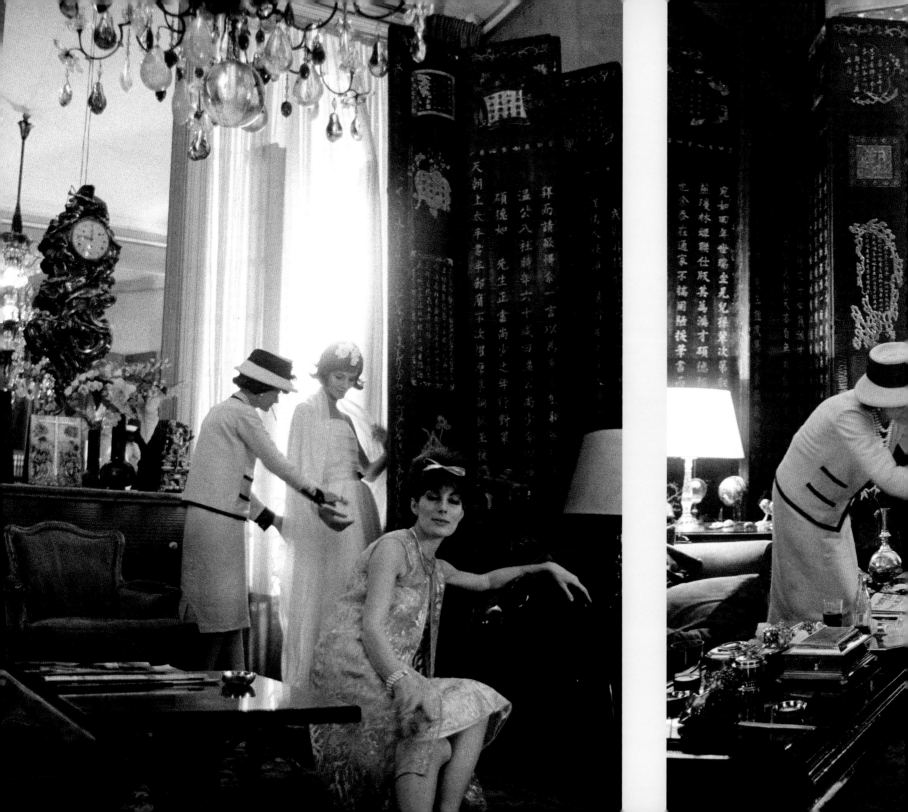

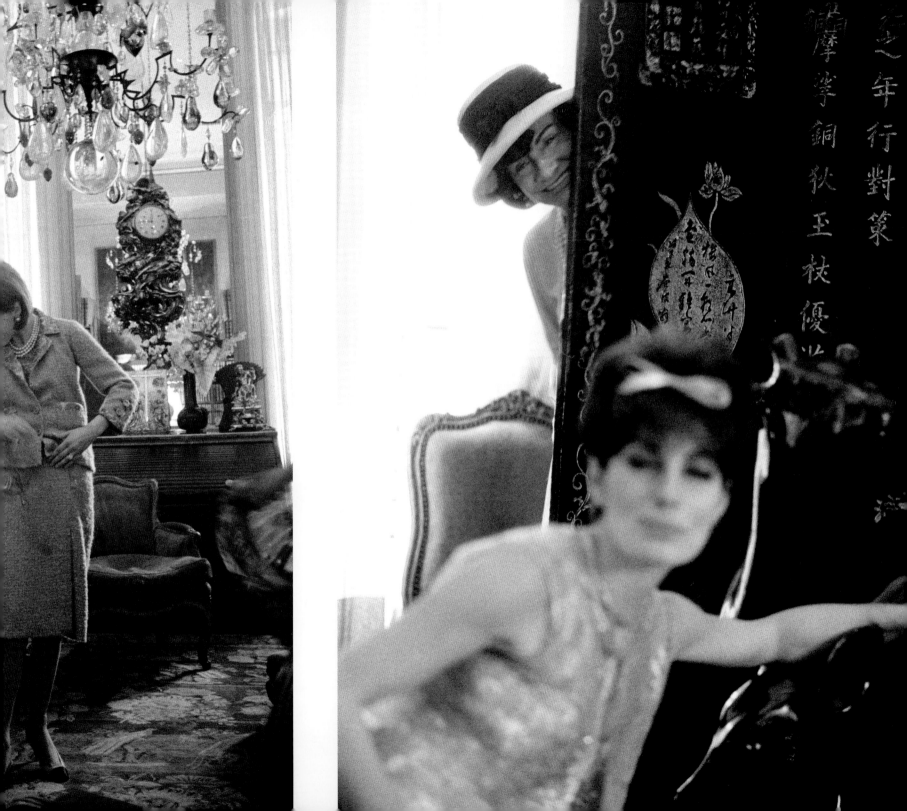

CONFRONTATION...

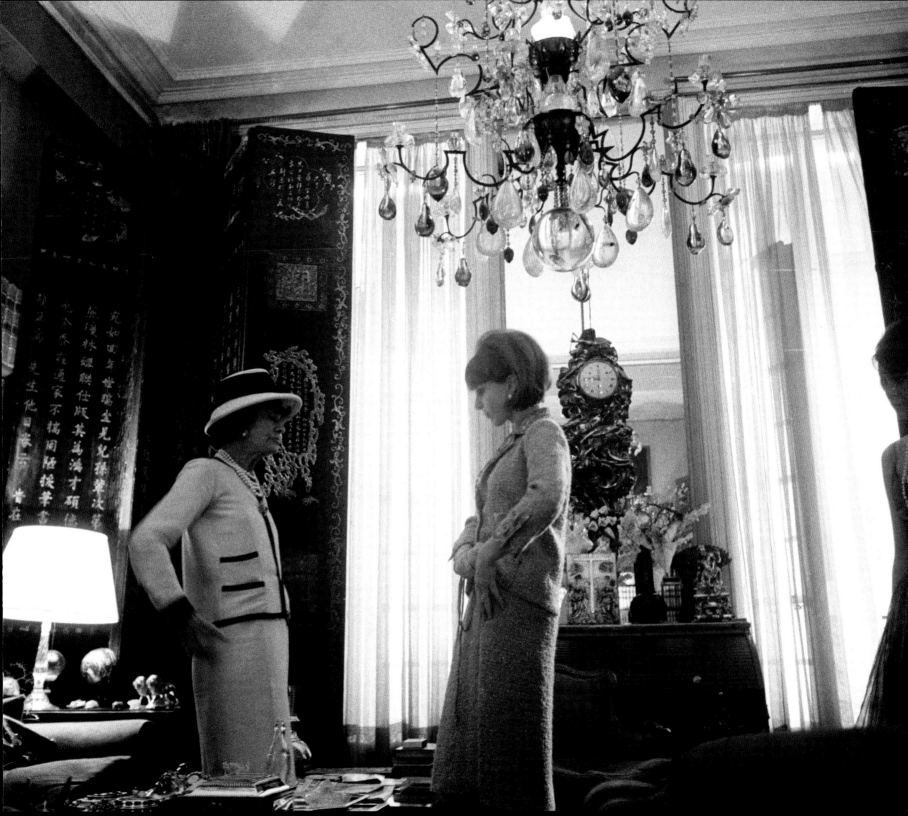

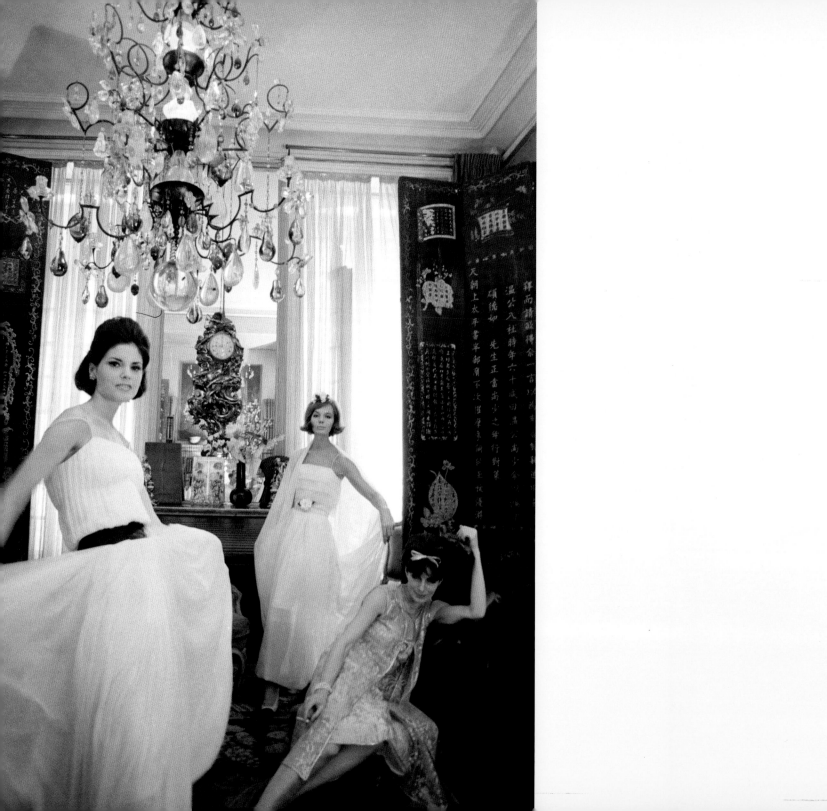

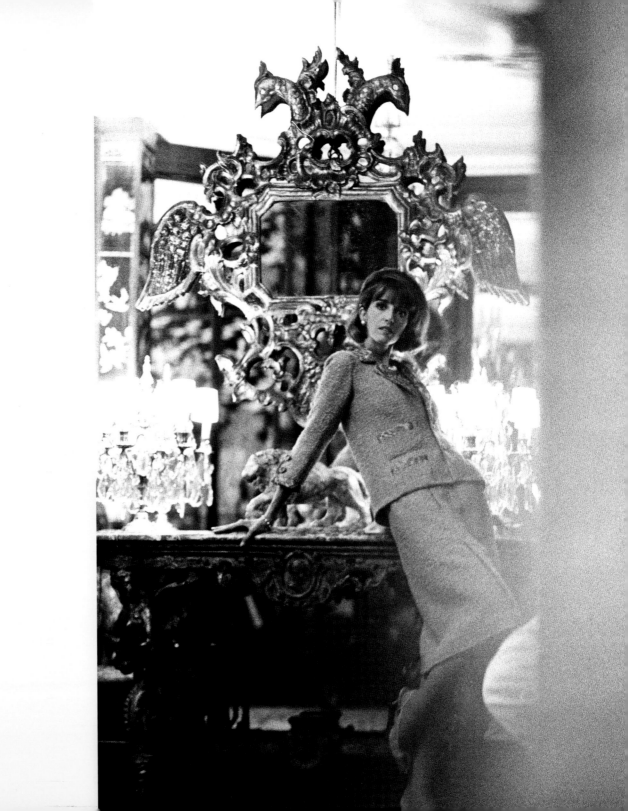

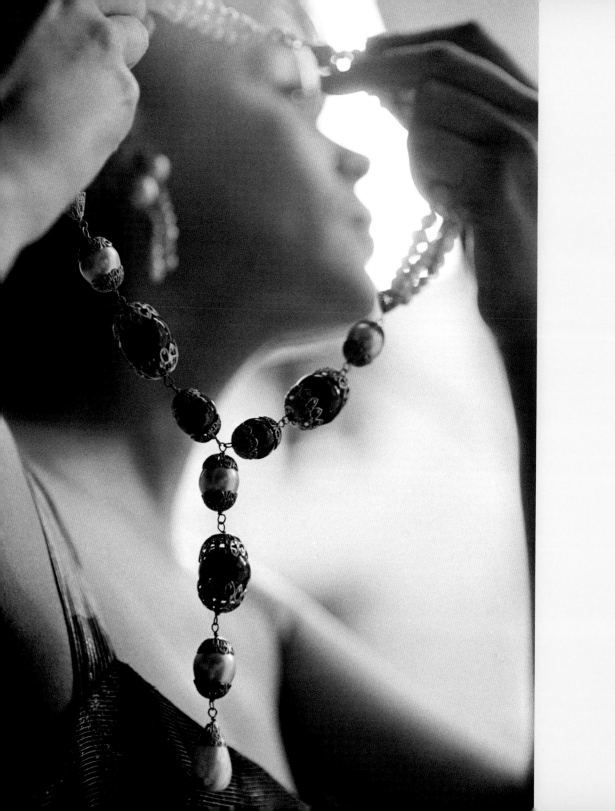

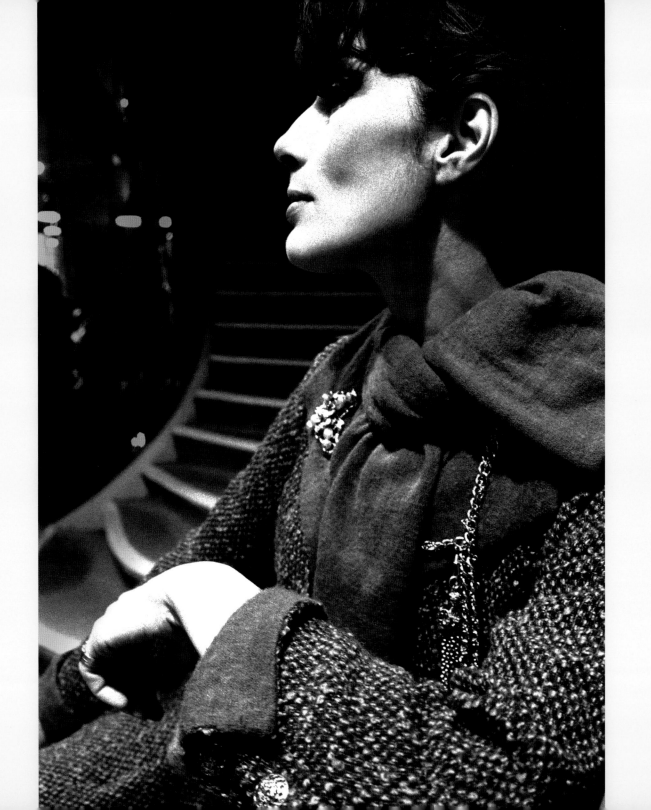

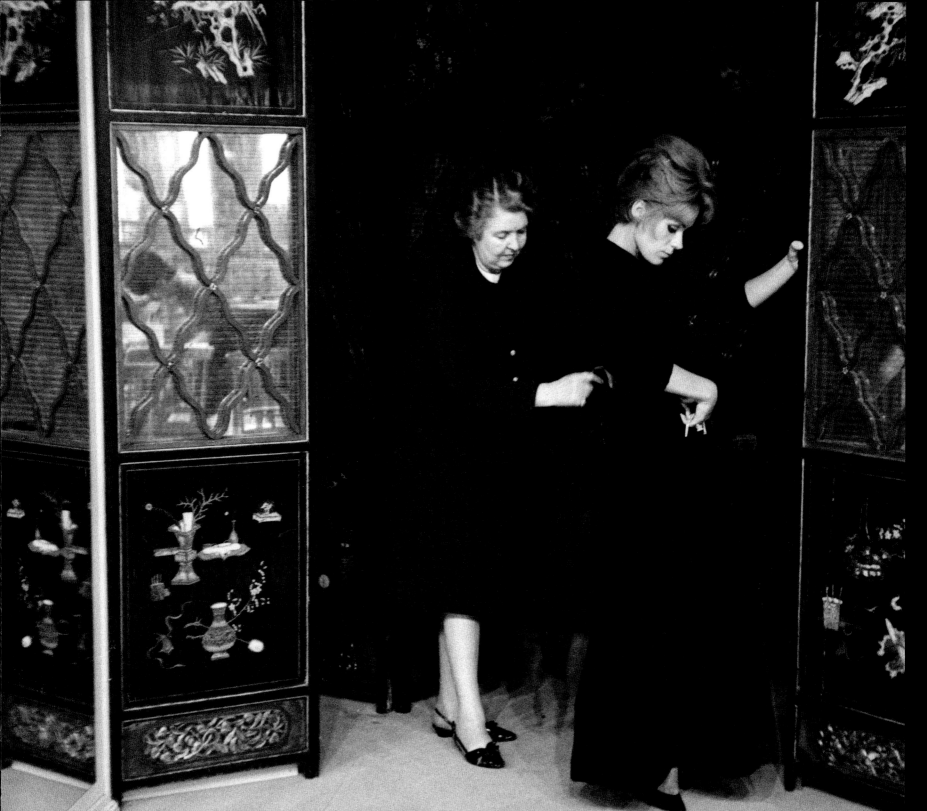

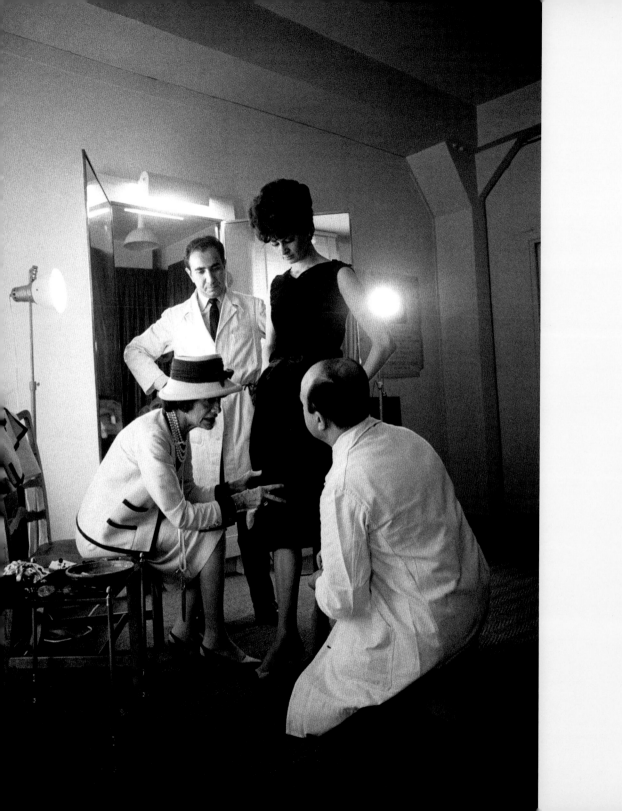

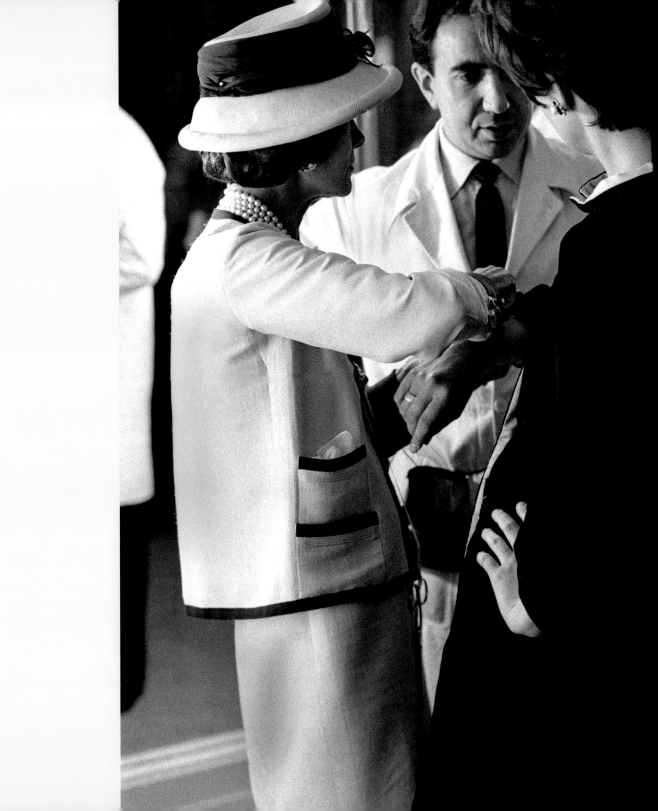

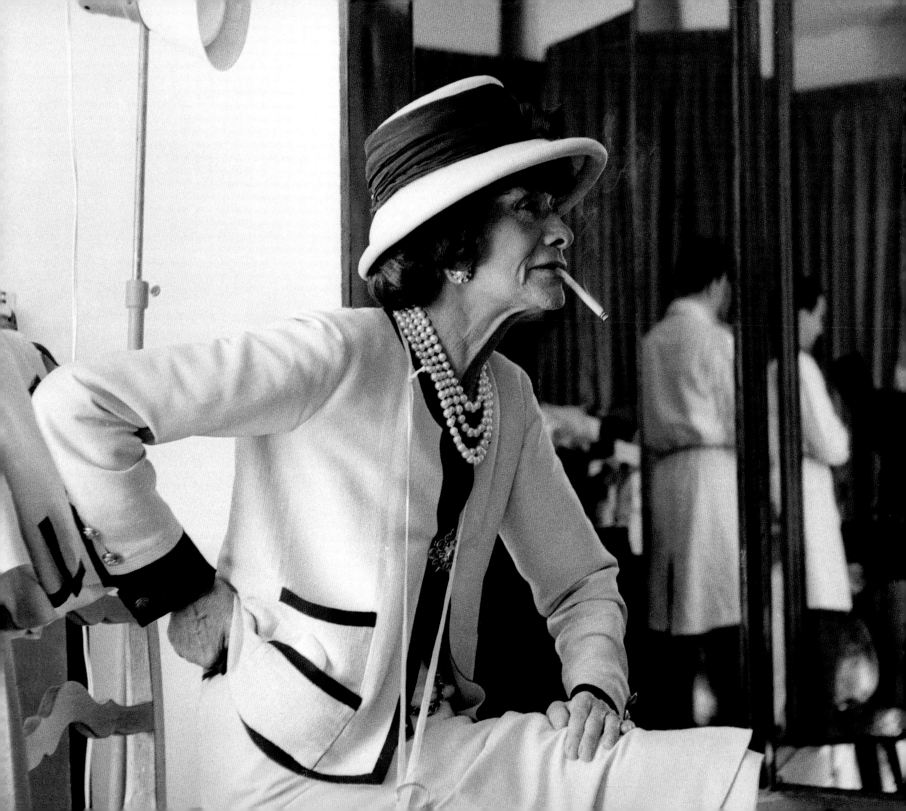

IT'S ALL ABOUT ATTITUDE...

THE FAMOUS FITTING OF THE SLEEVE...

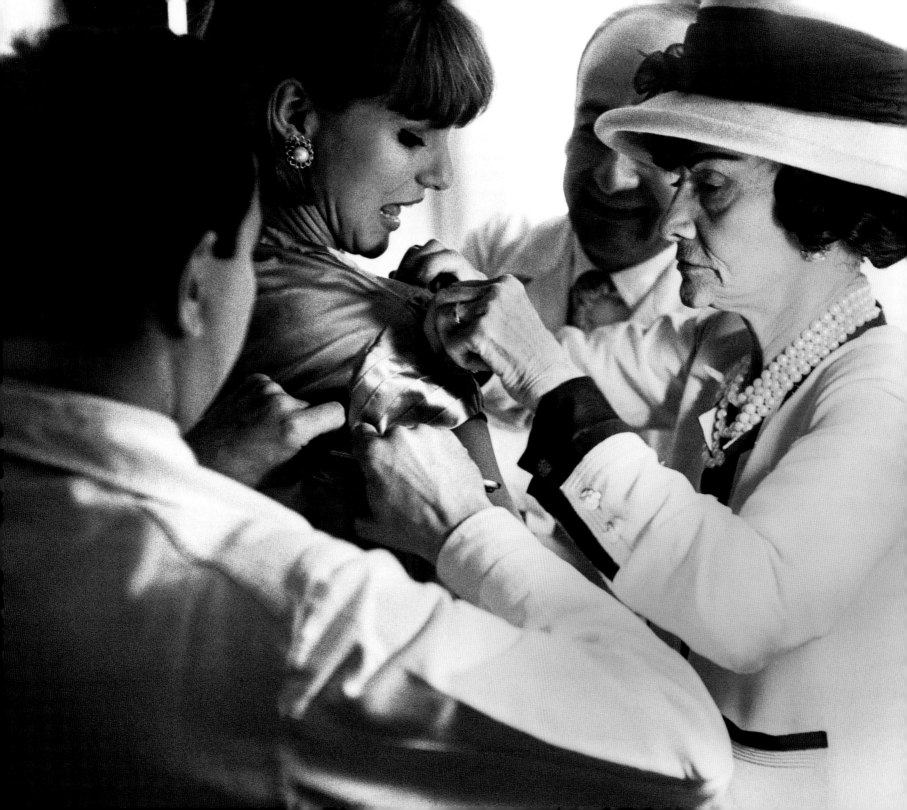

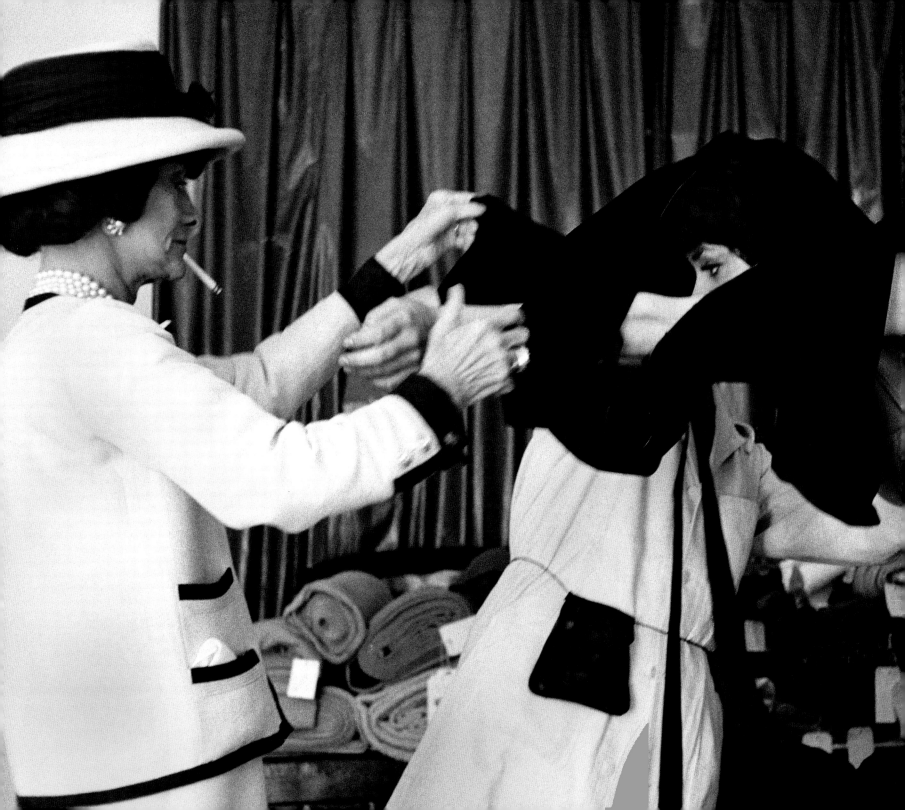

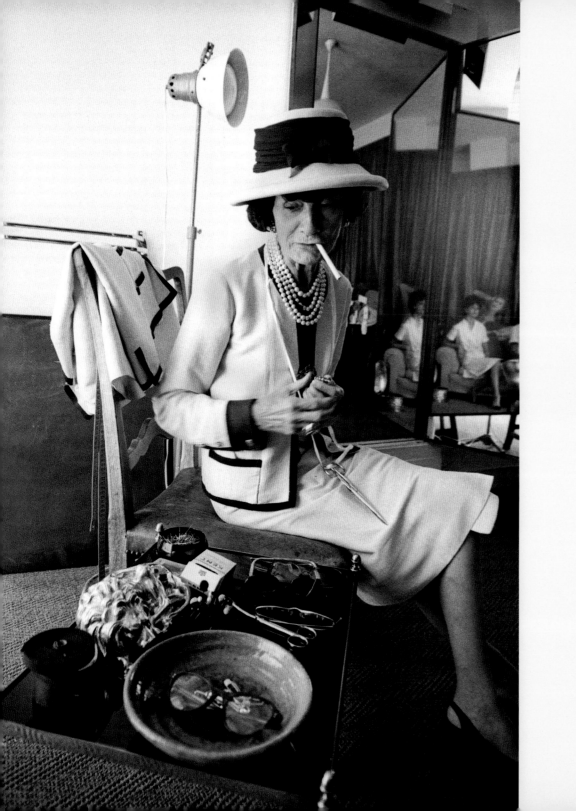

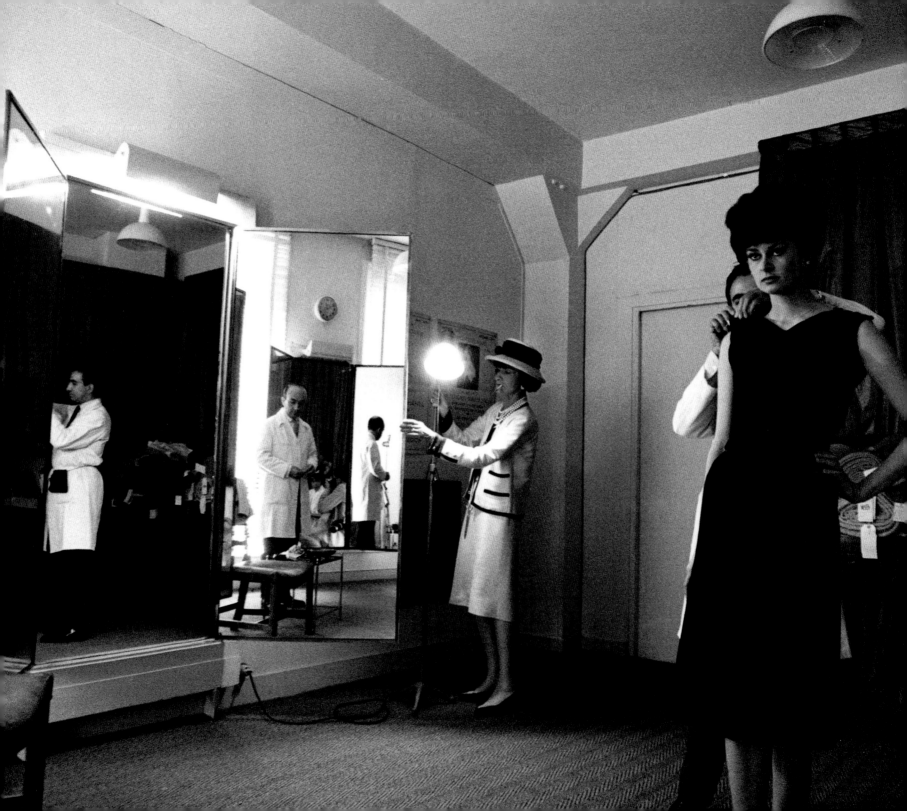

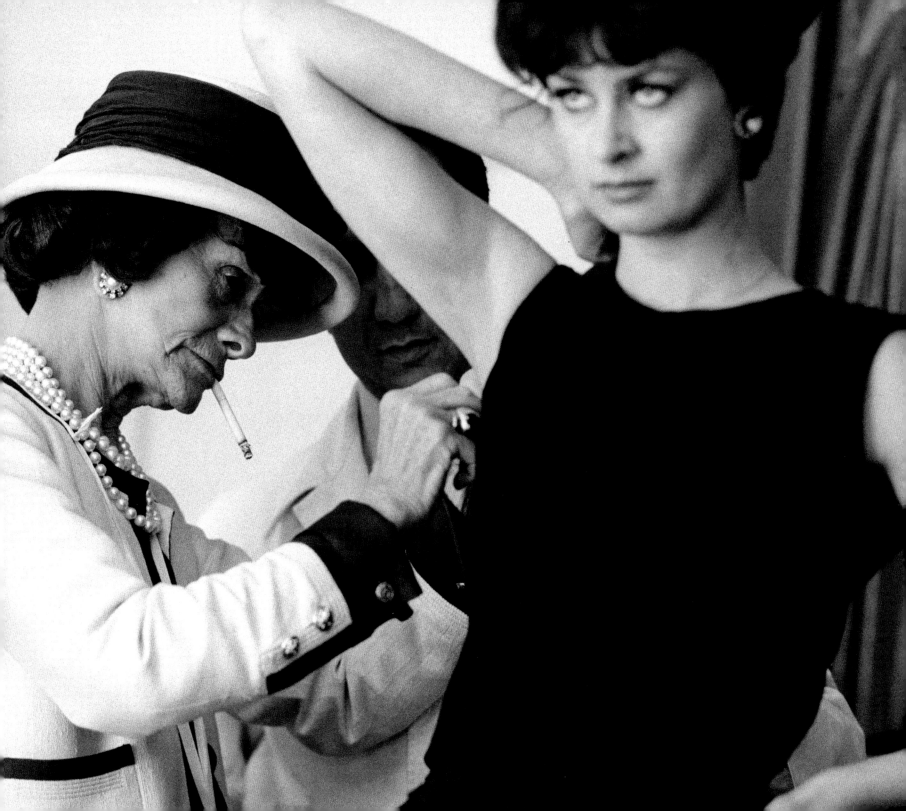

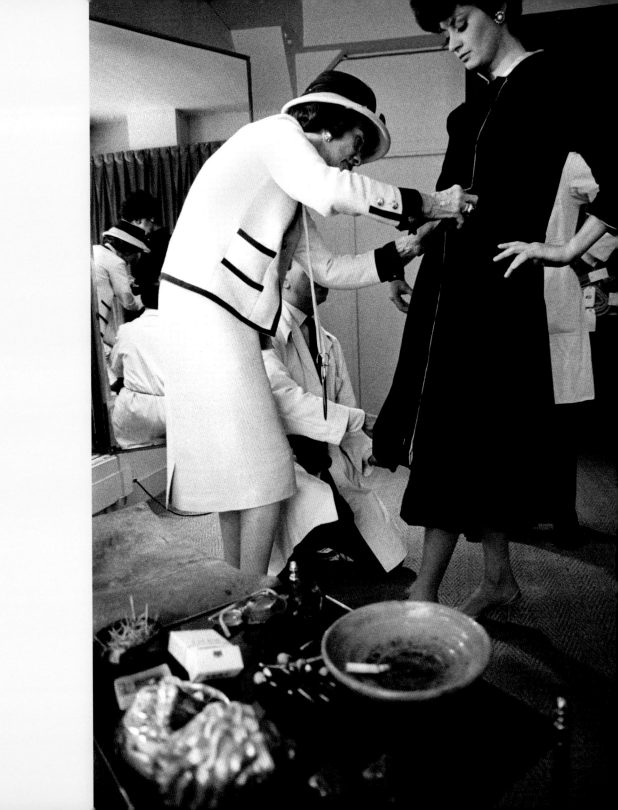

THE SPECTRE OF THE PAST...

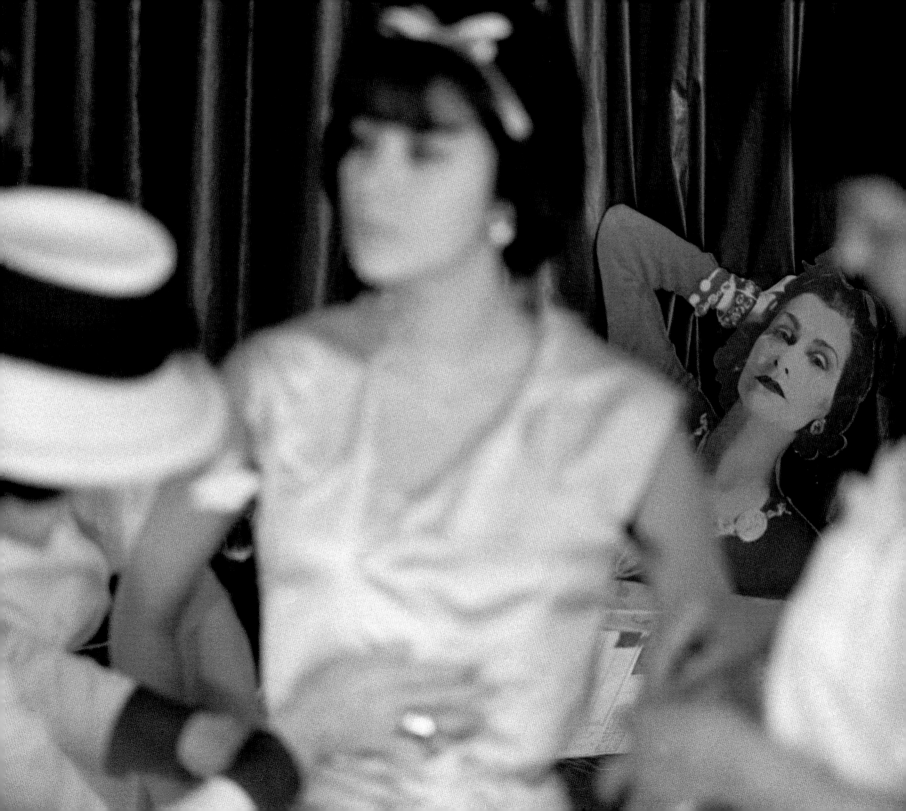

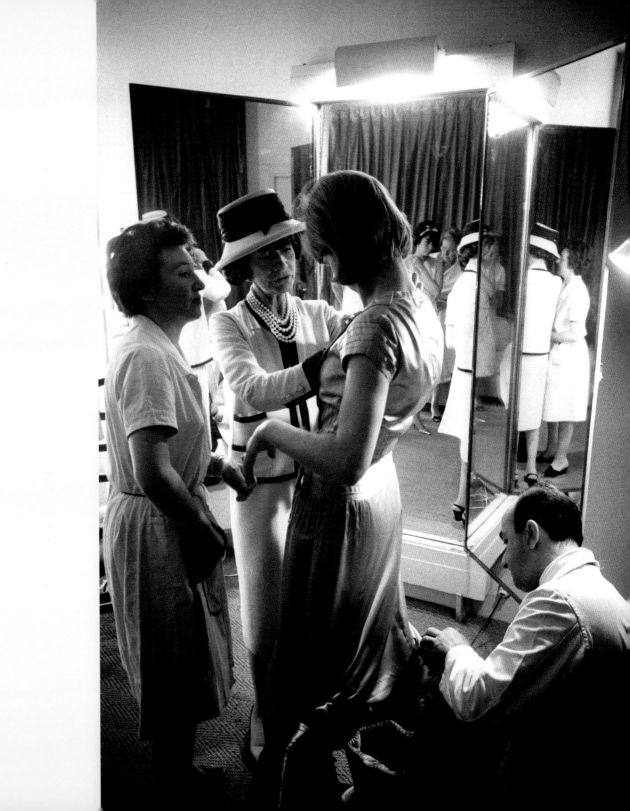

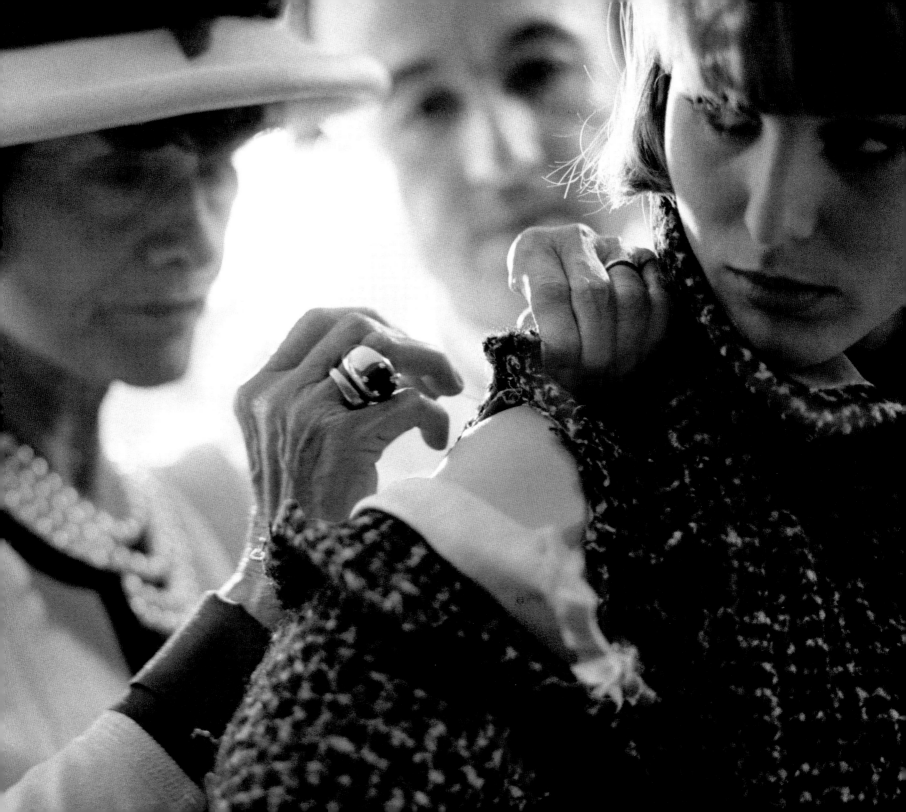

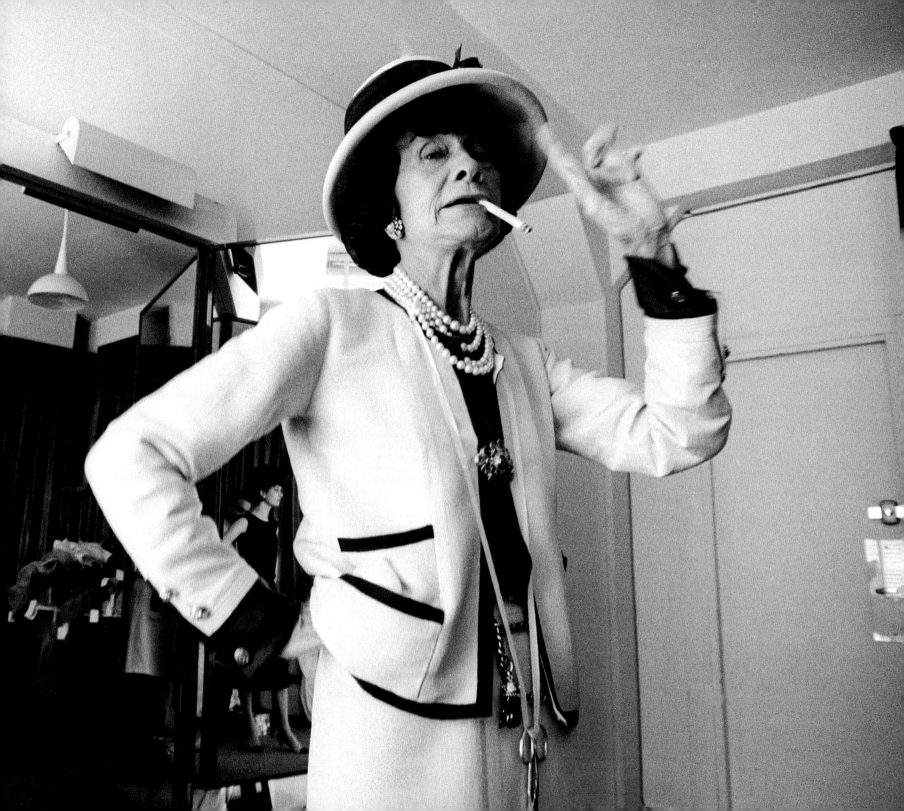

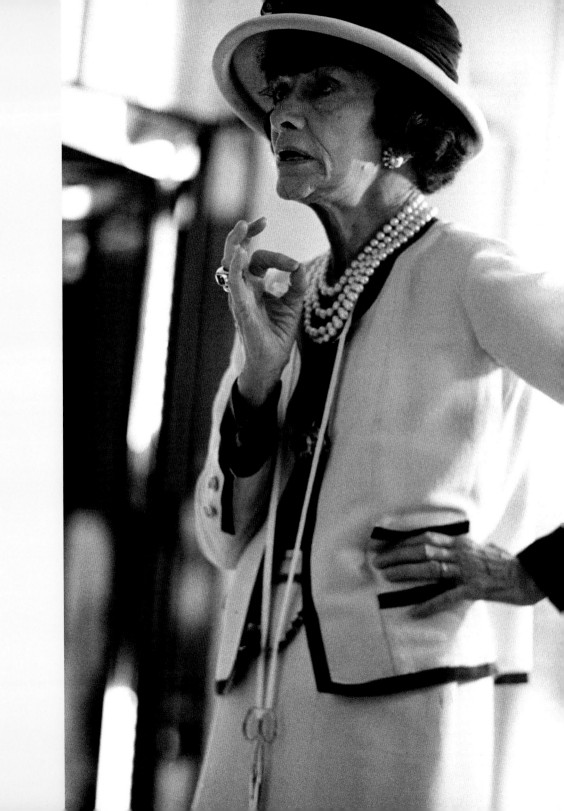

LESSON OF STYLE

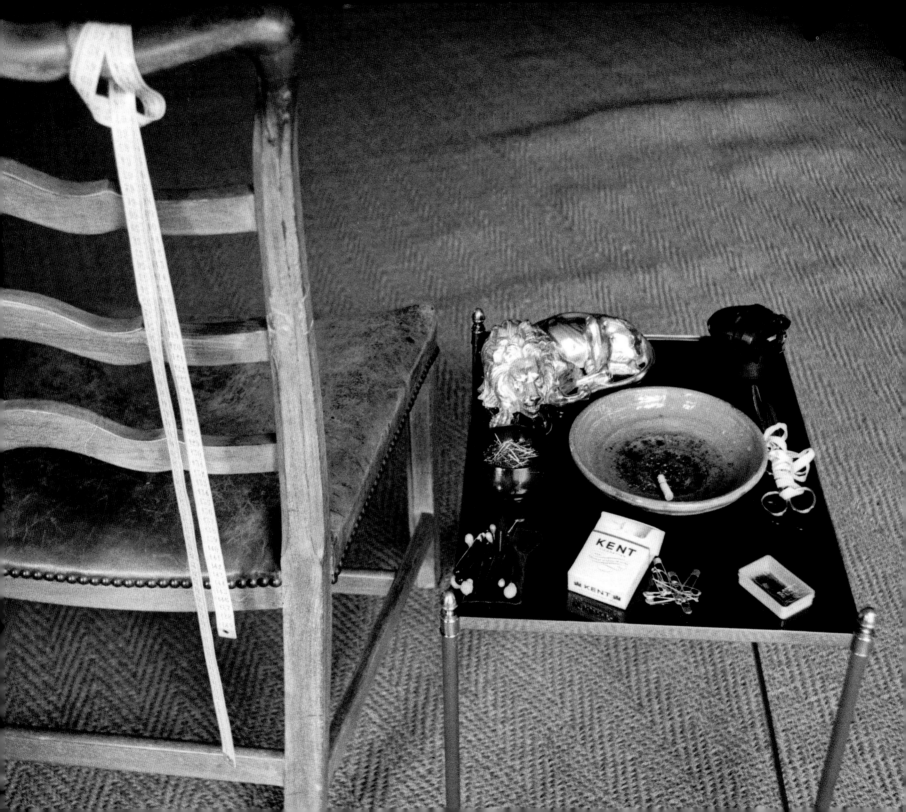

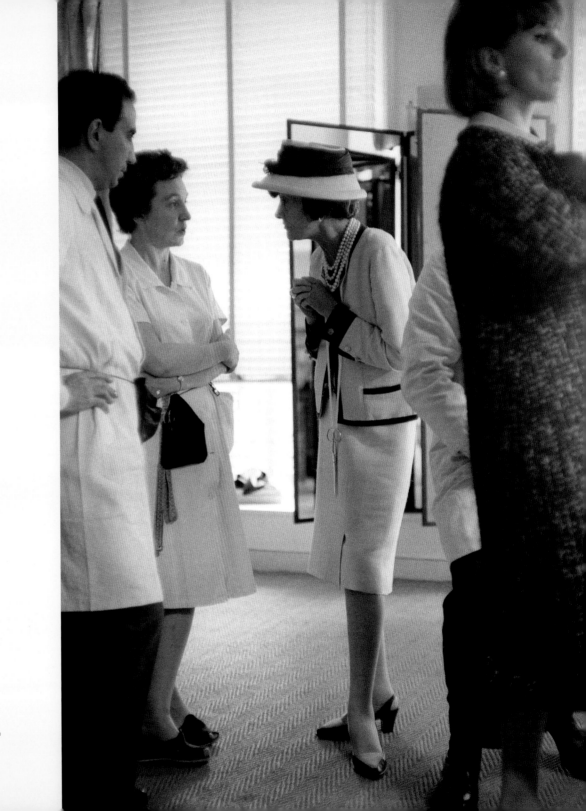

YOU SEE WHAT I MEAN...

THE "CABINE"

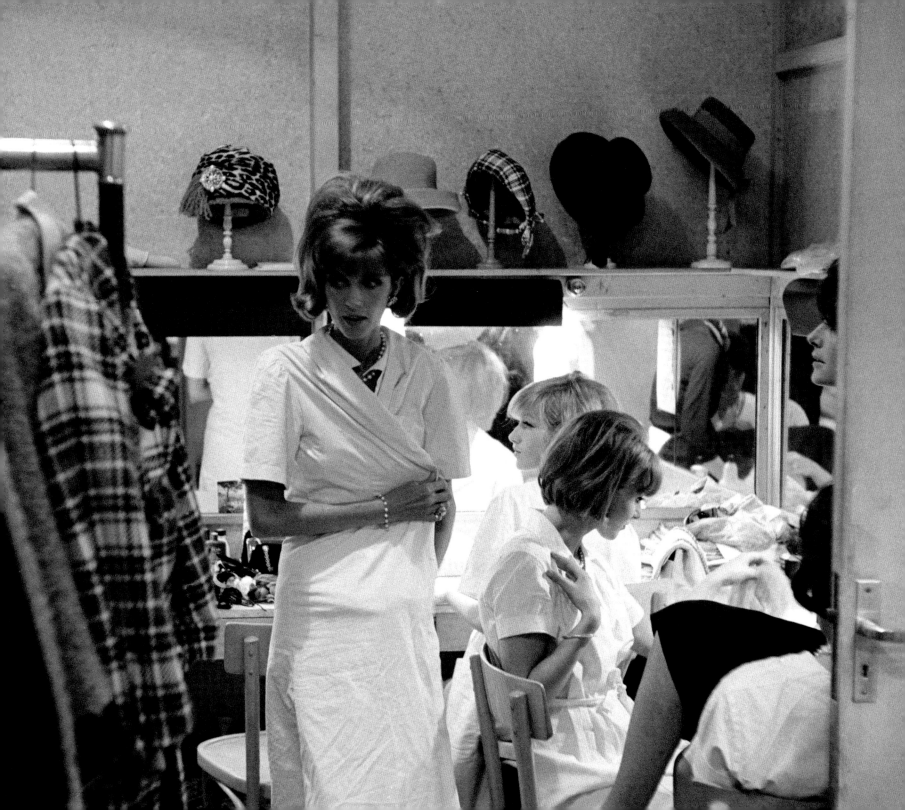

KEEP SMILING

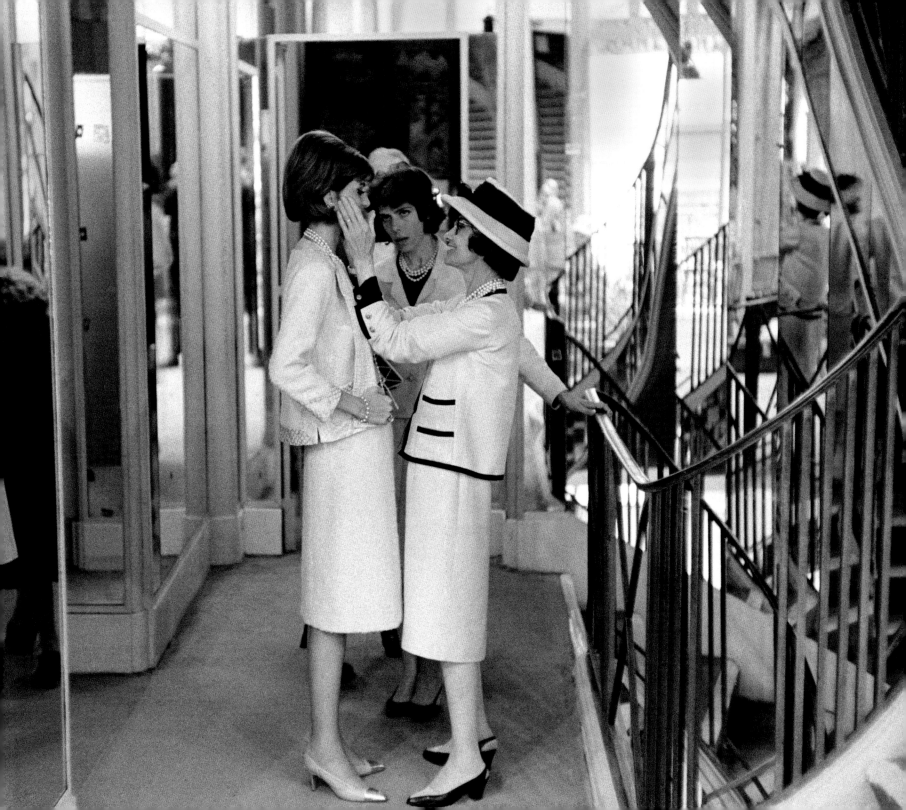

BETTINA GRAZIANI AND ART BUCHWALD

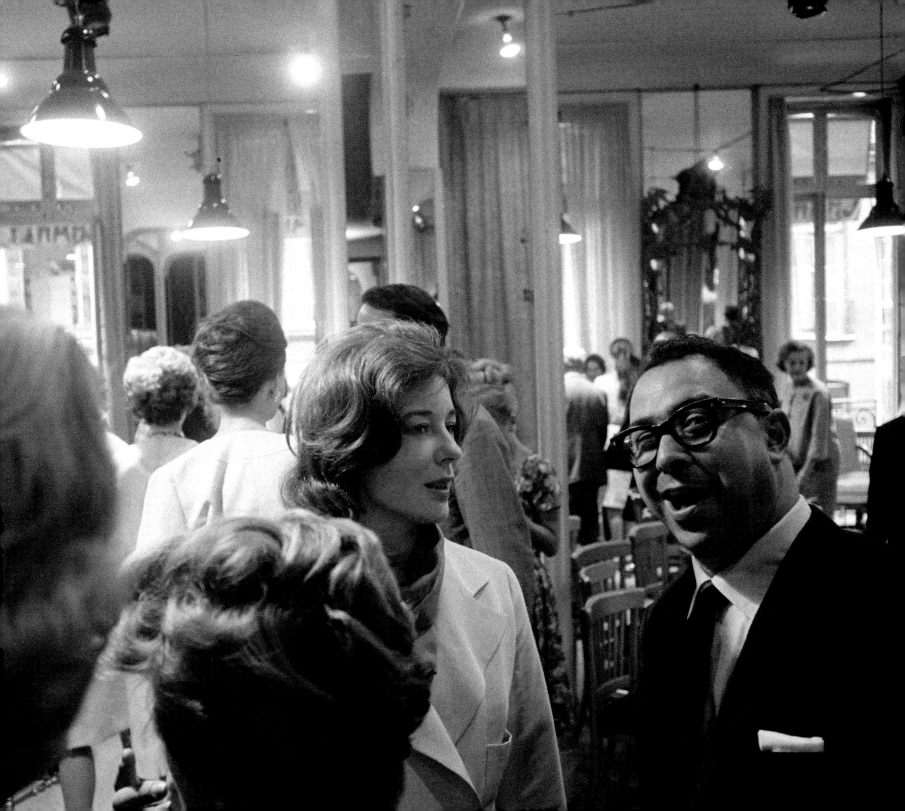

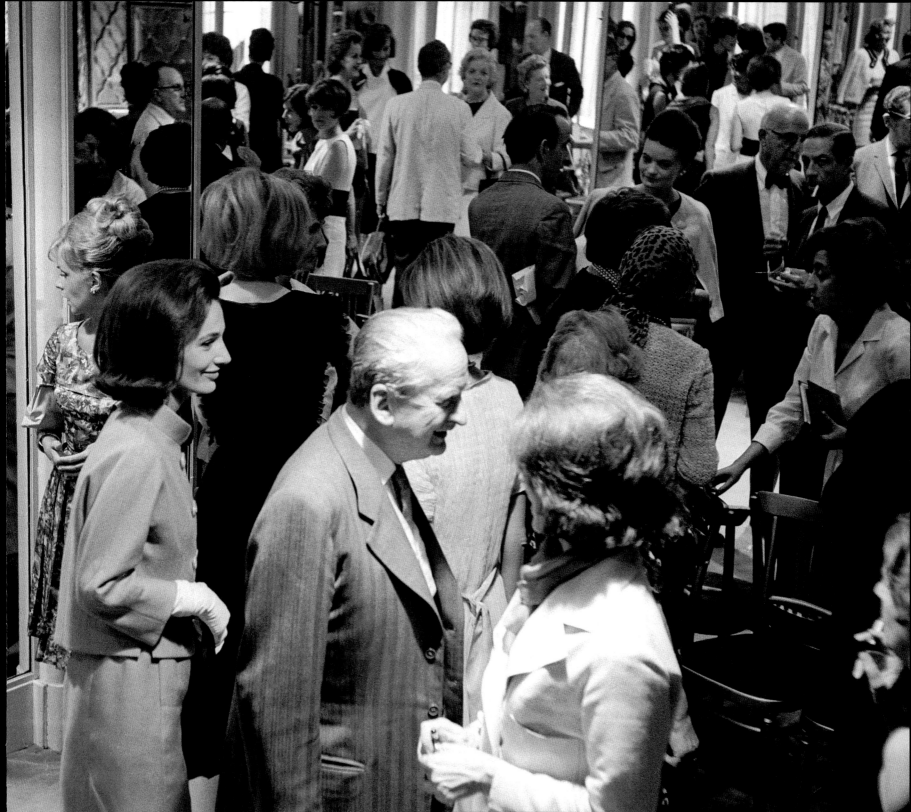

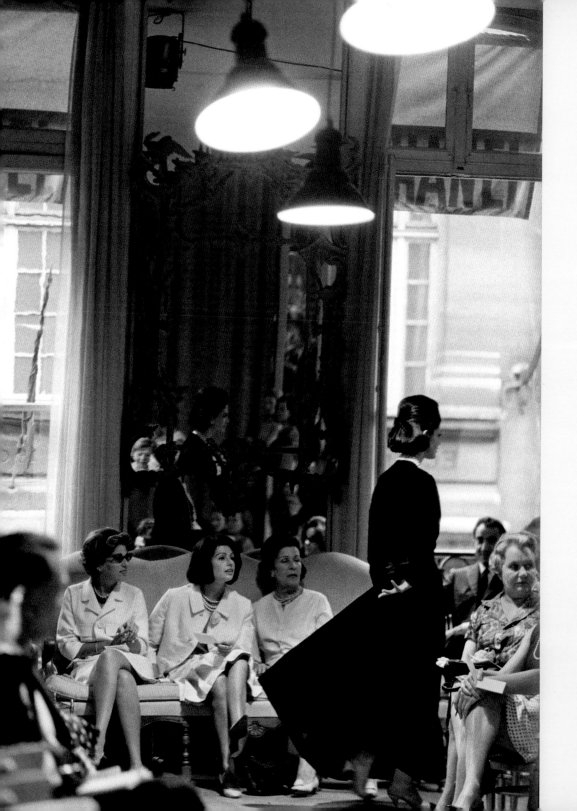

FRONT ROW

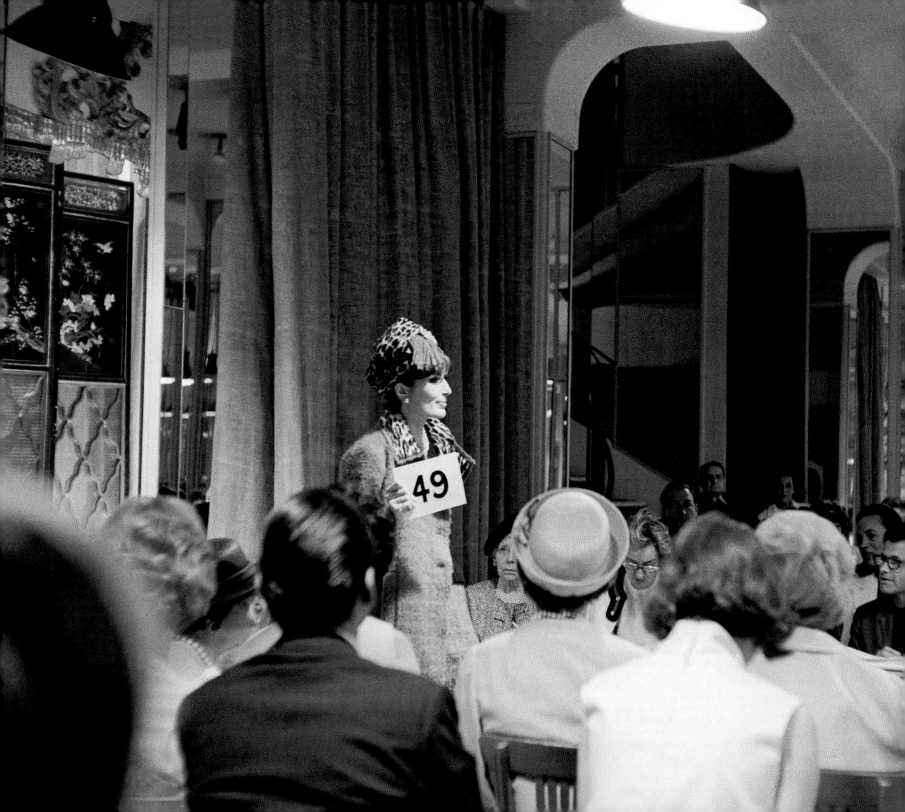

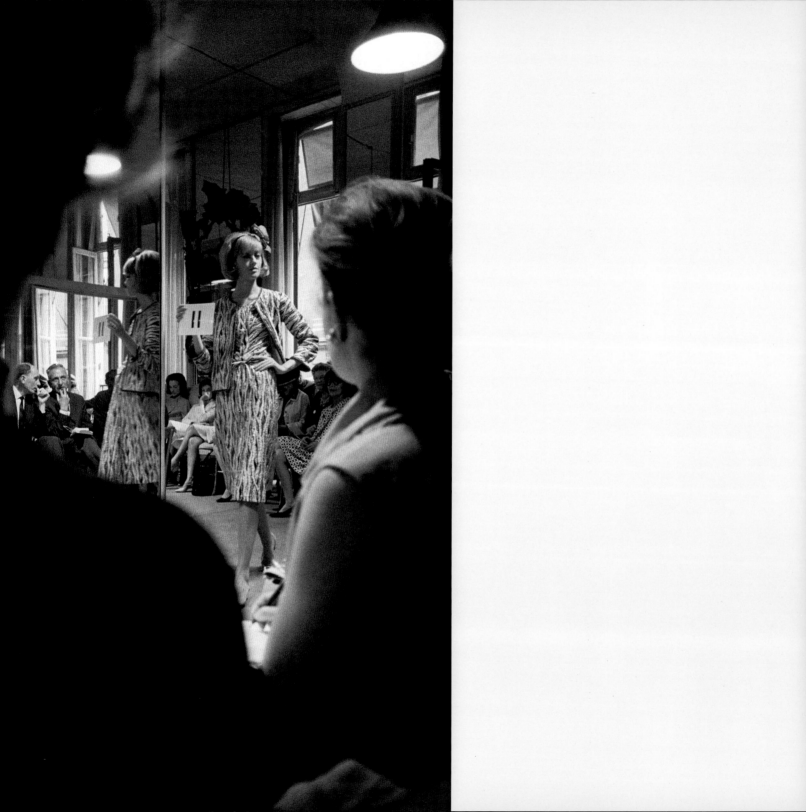

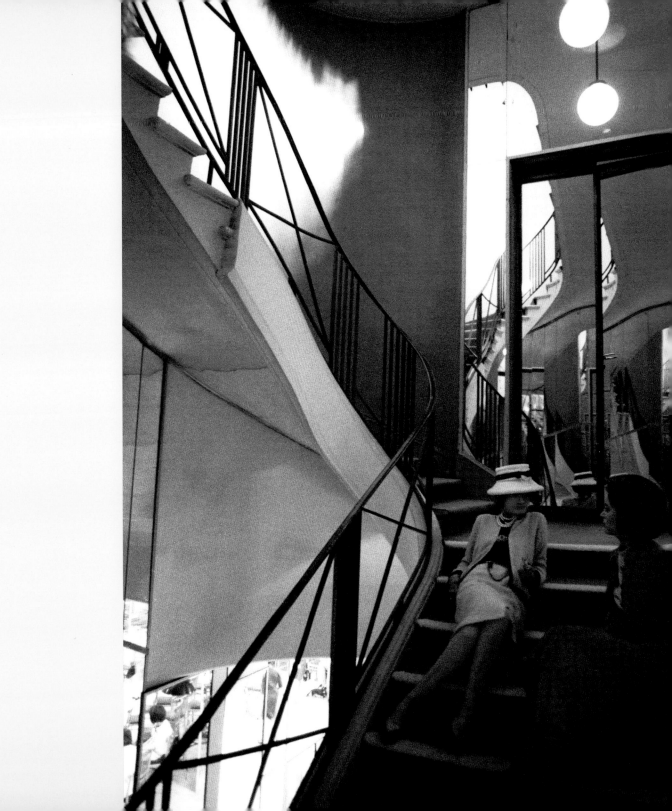

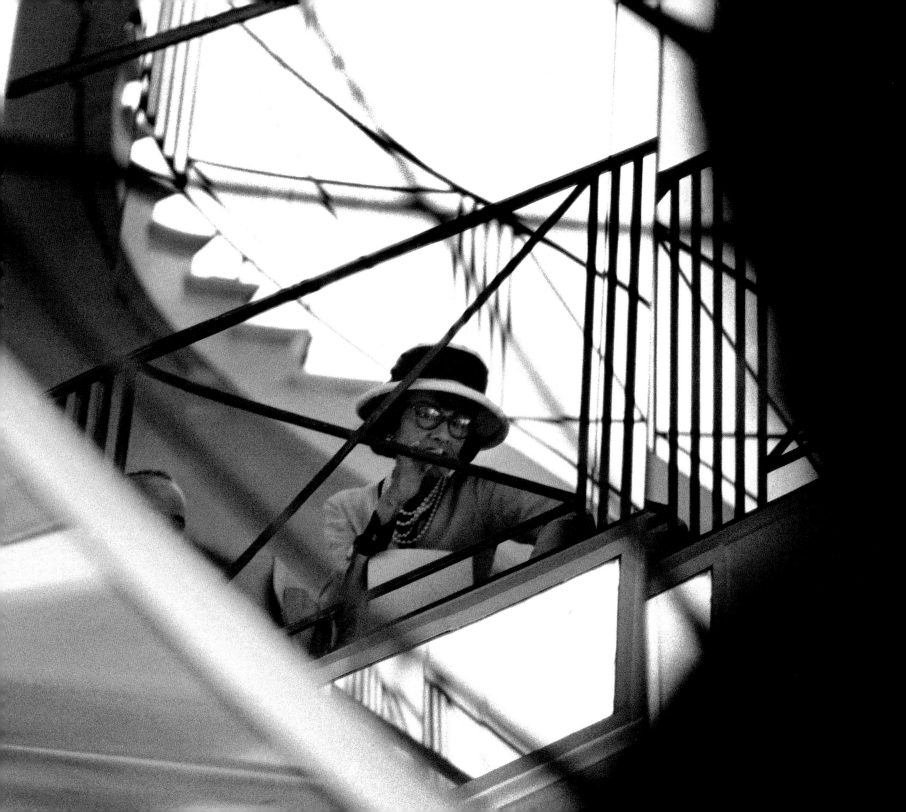

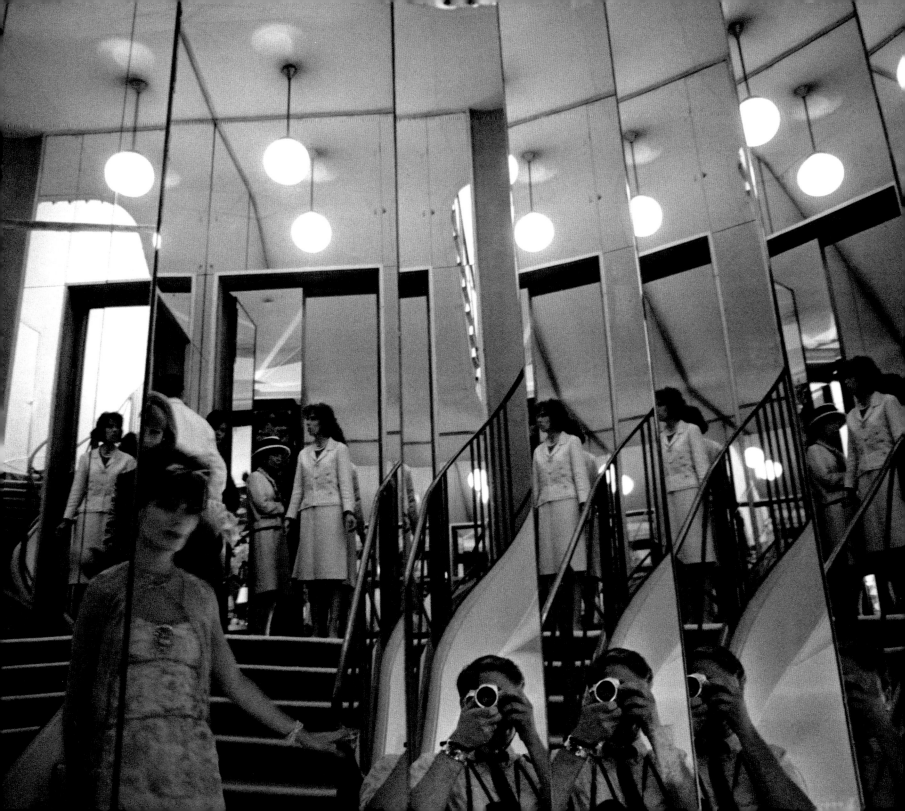

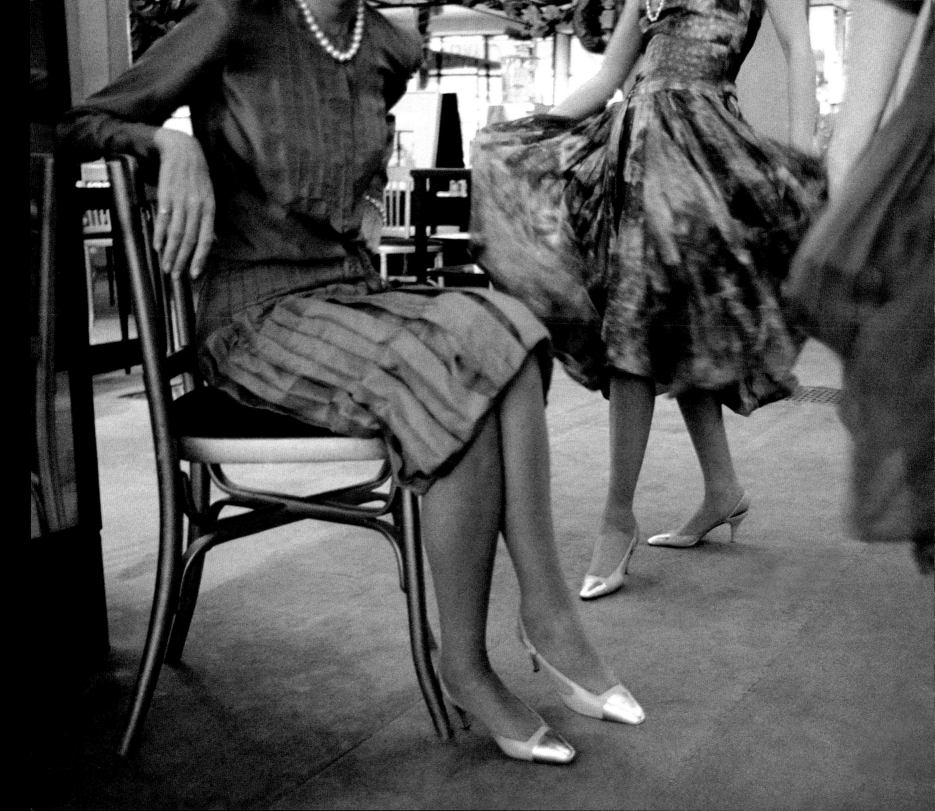

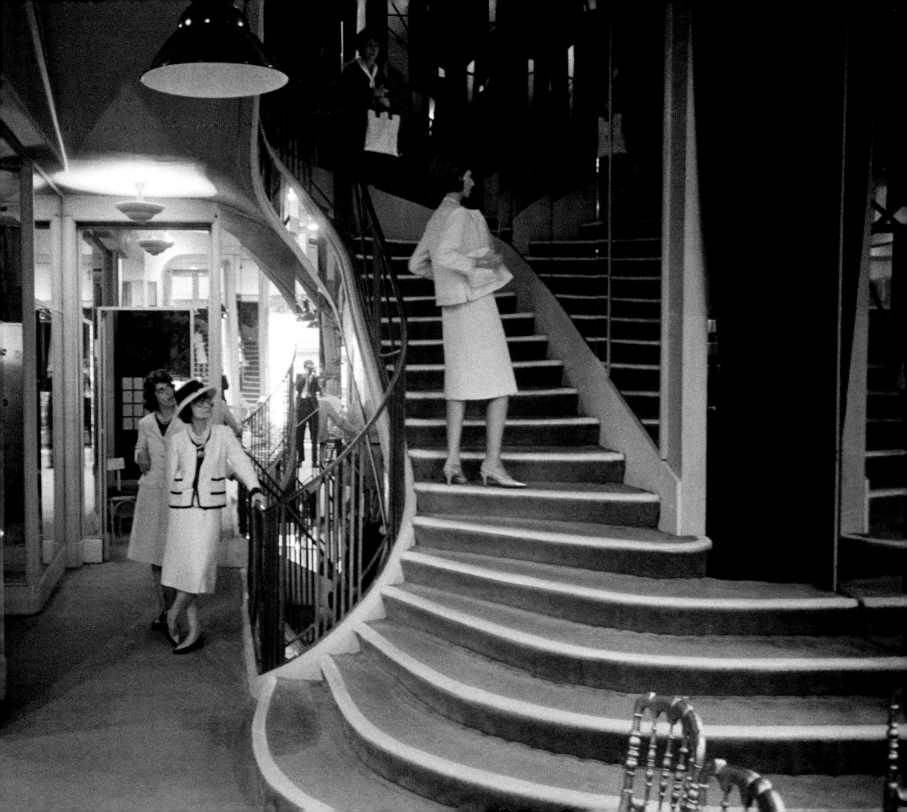

FINALE OF THE SHOW

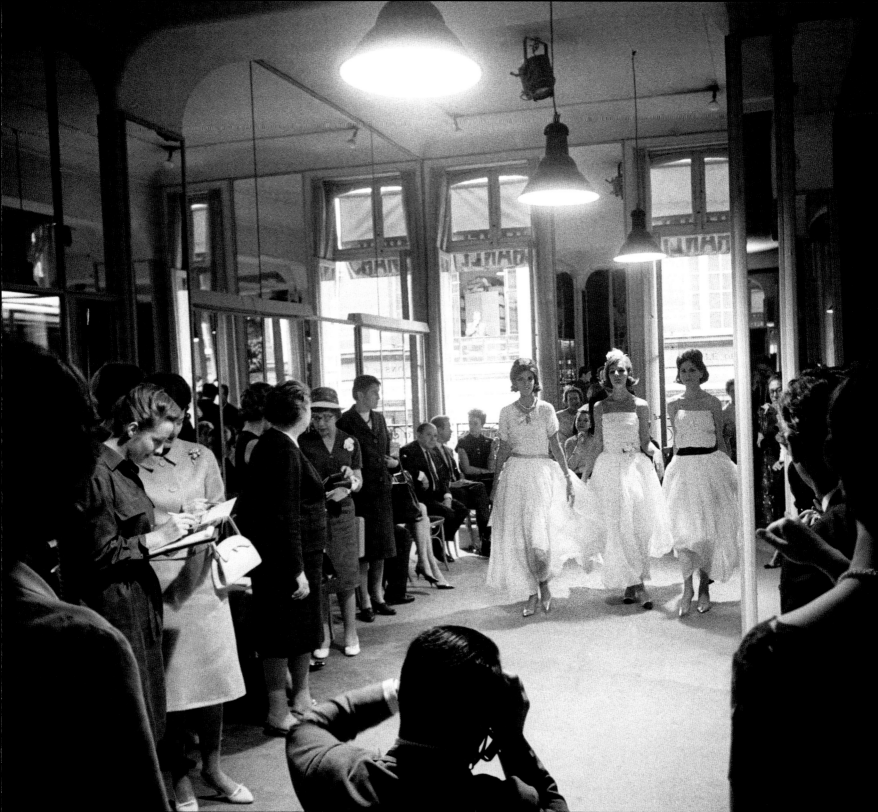

IN THE CENTRE: RICHARD AVEDON

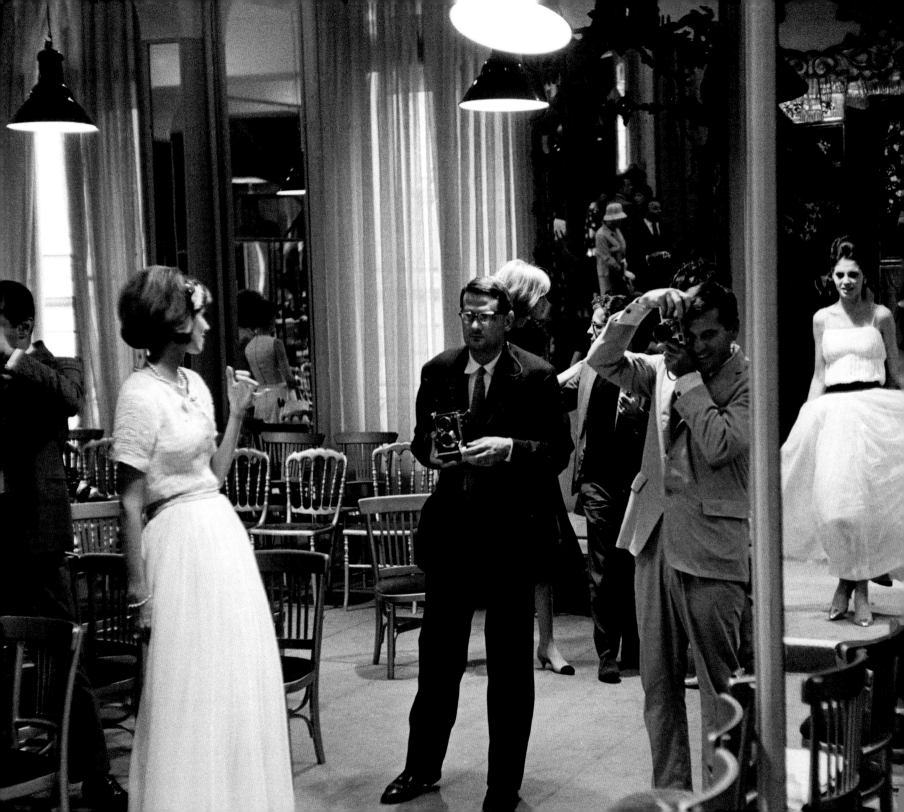

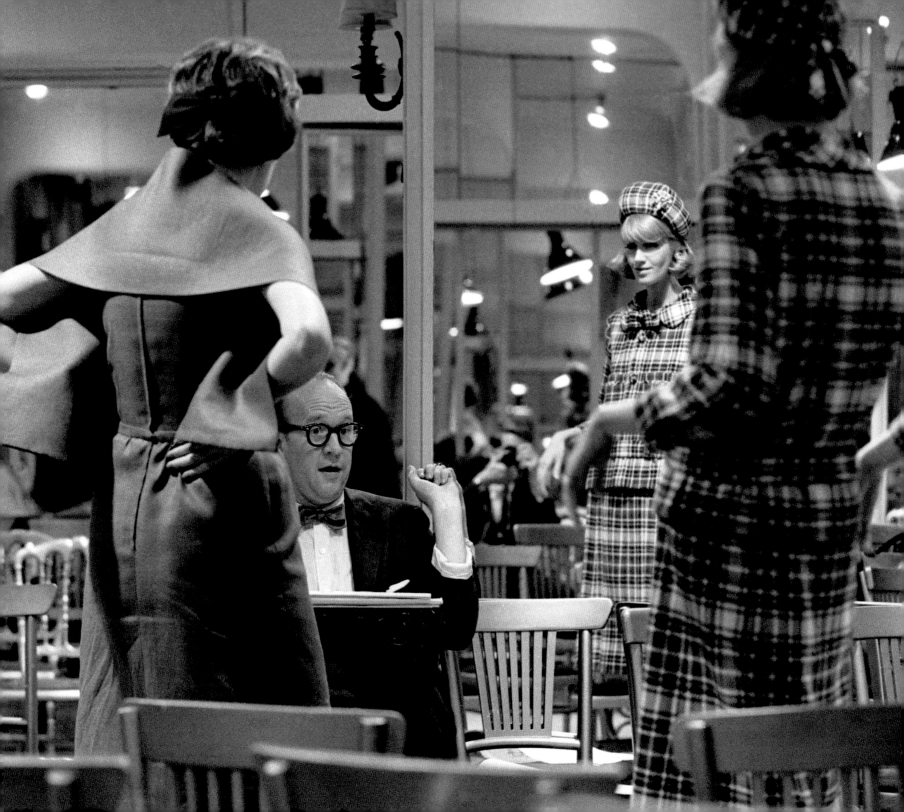

BACKSTAGE

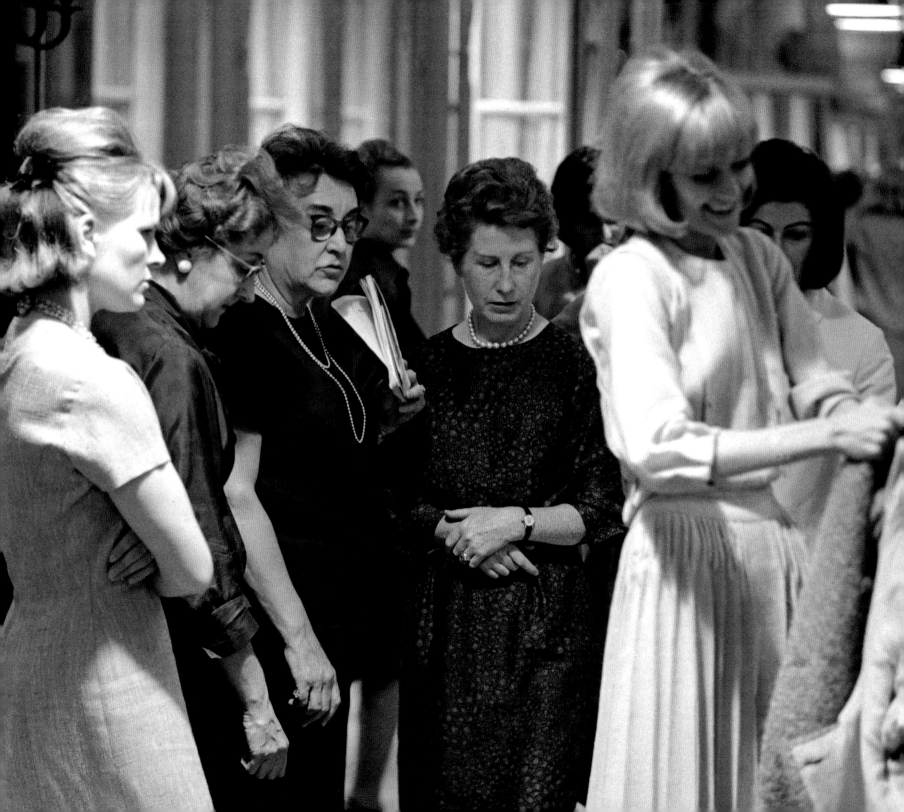

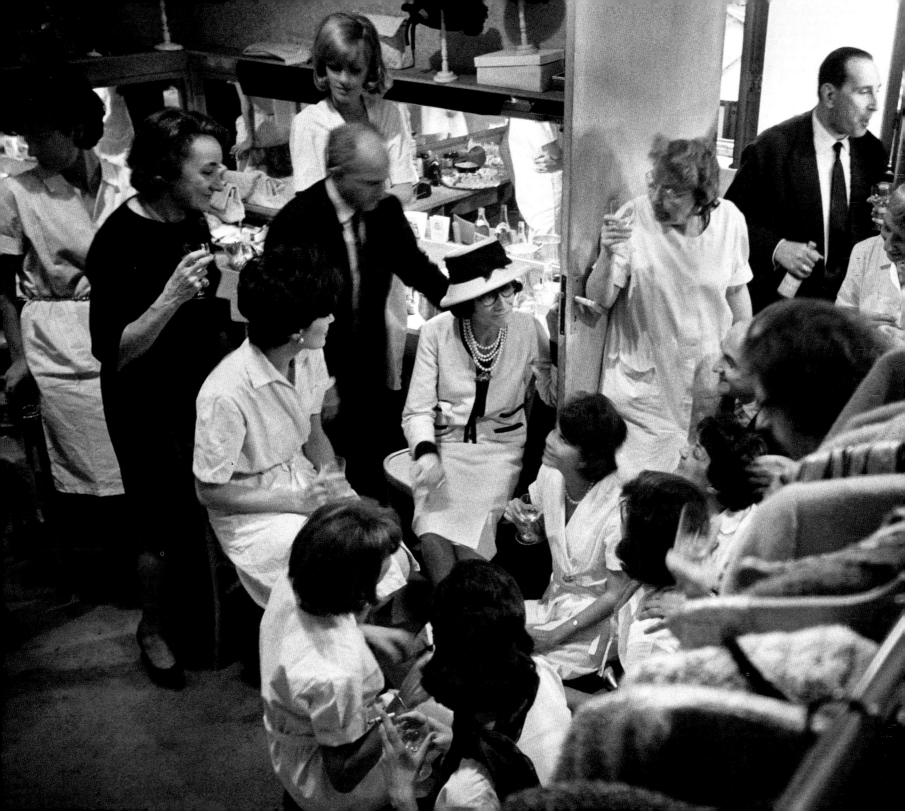

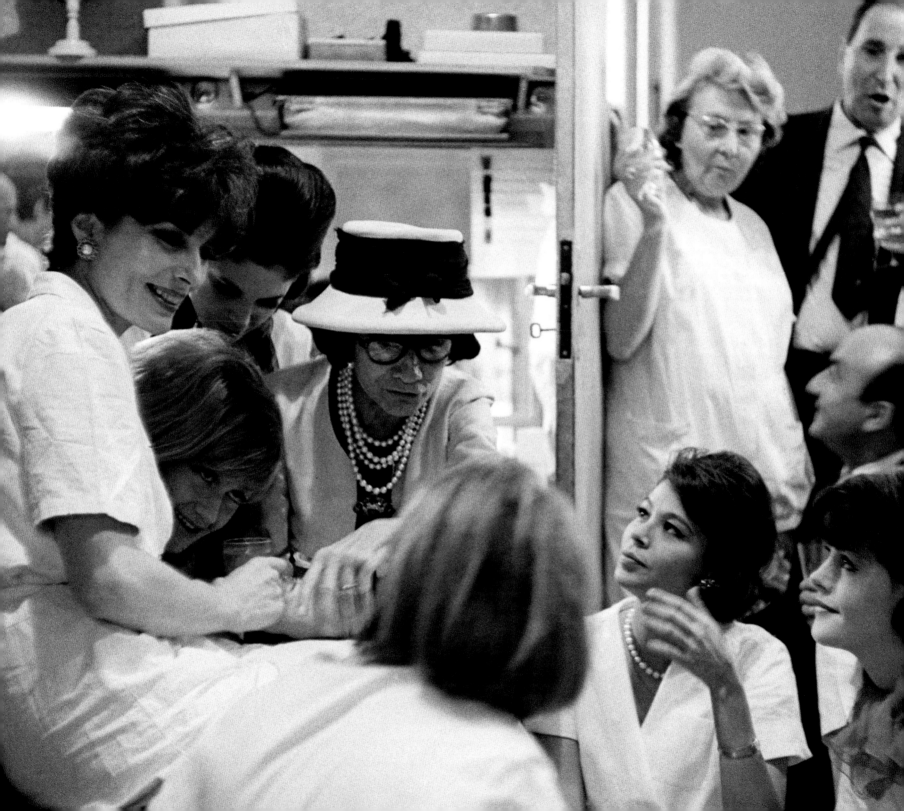

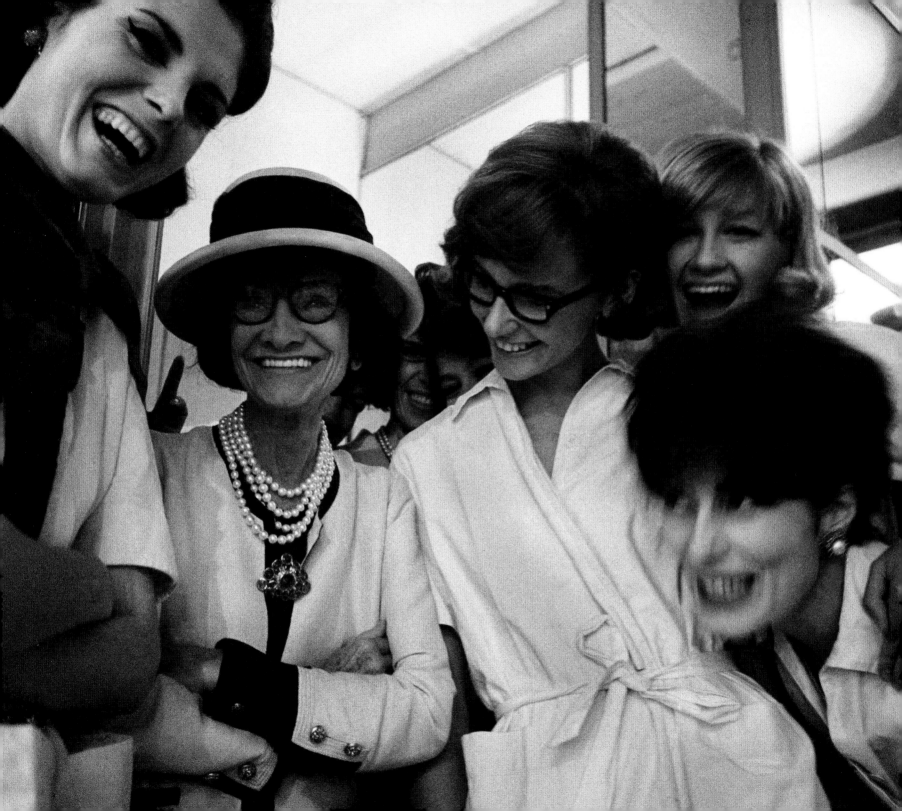

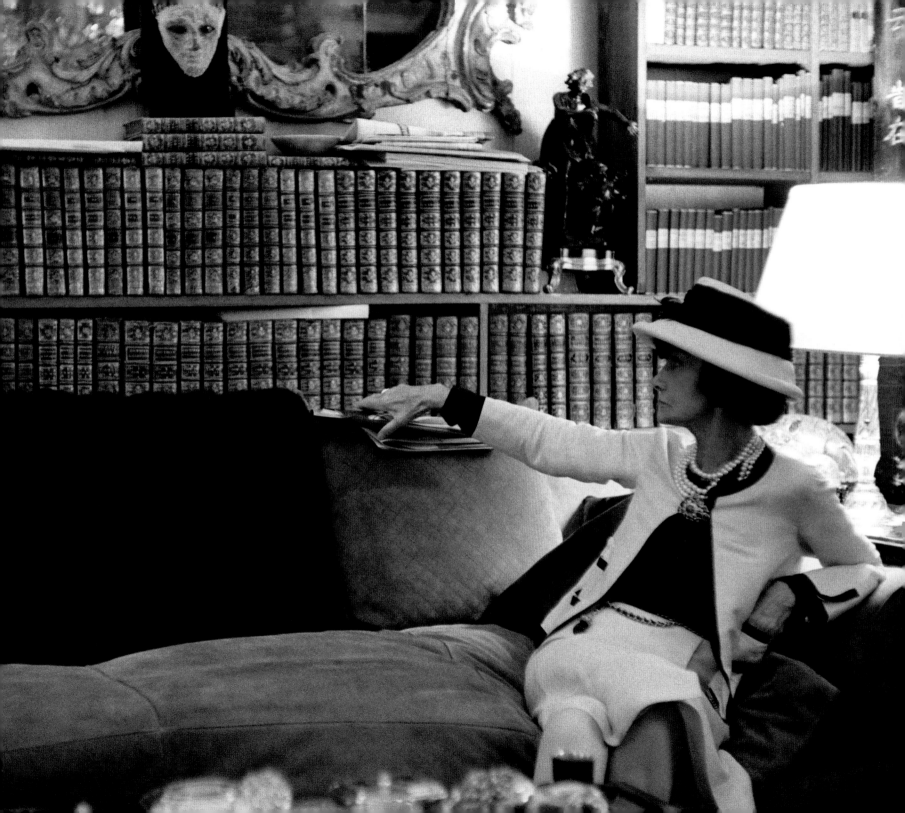

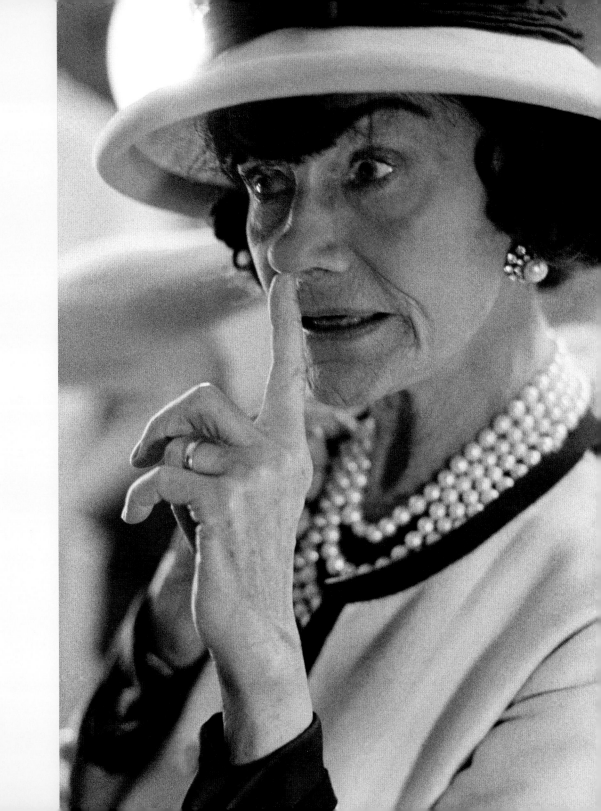

I TOLD YOU!

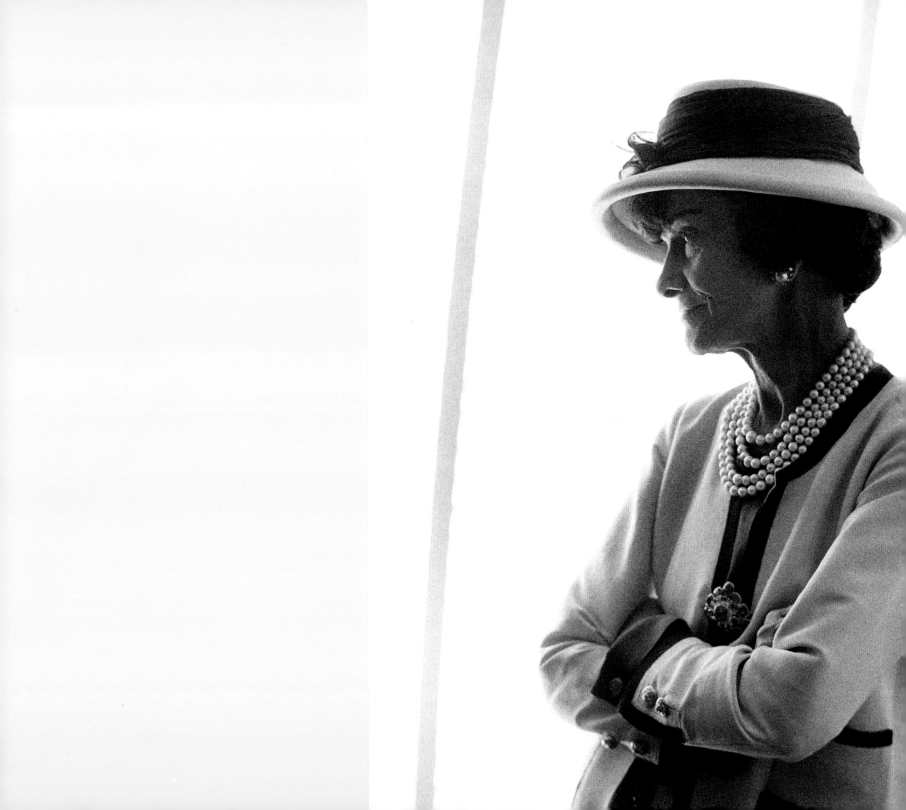

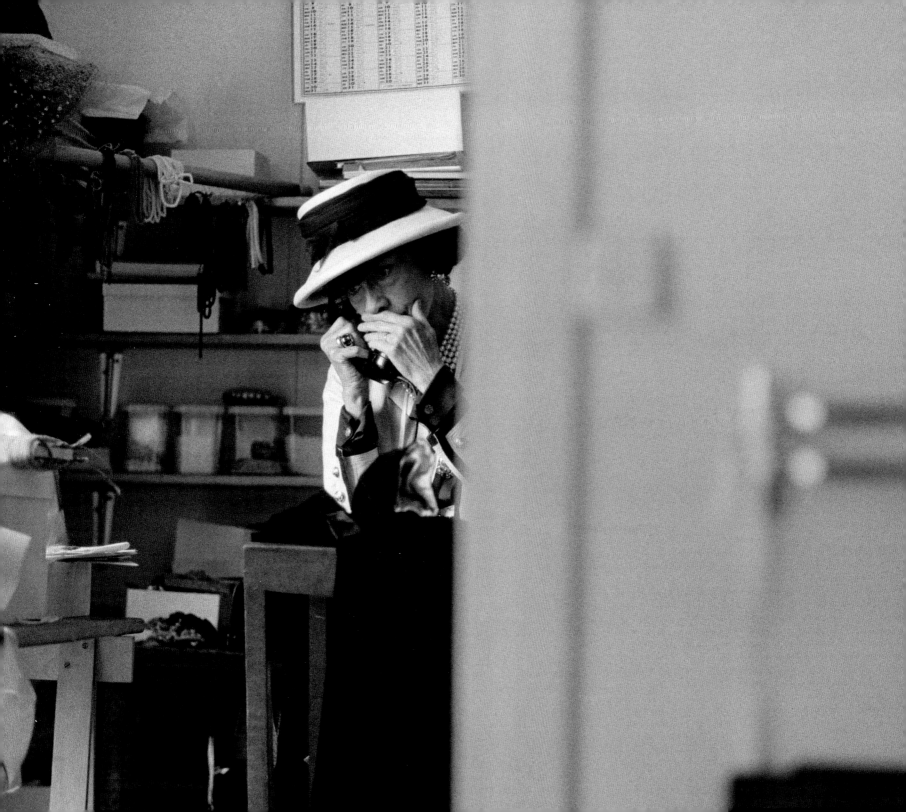

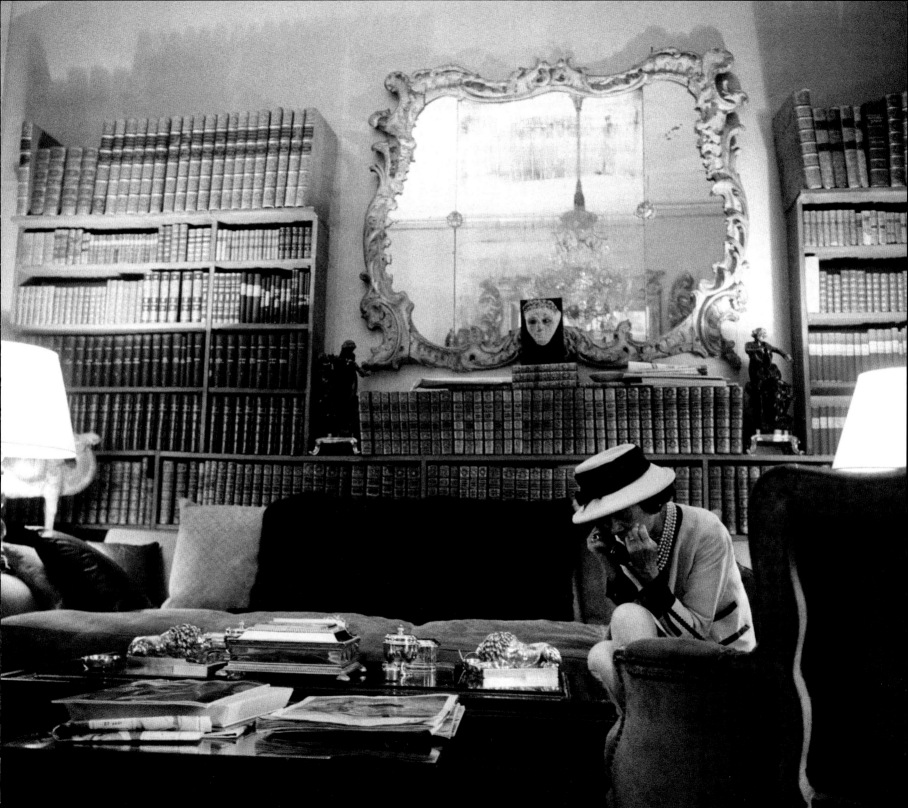

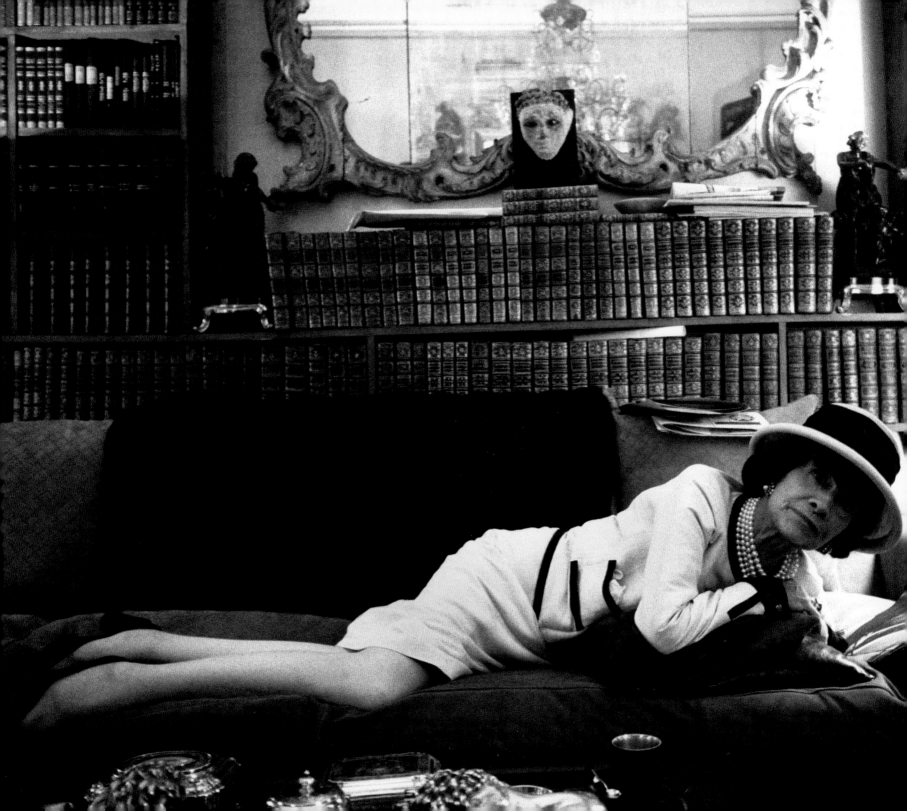

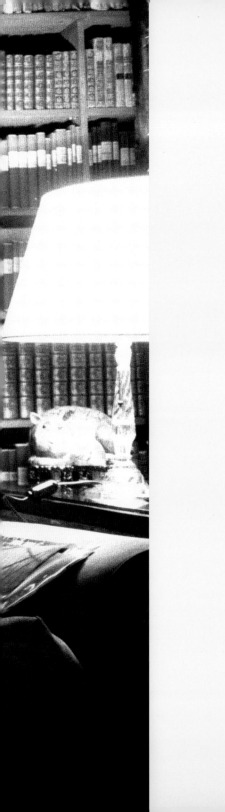

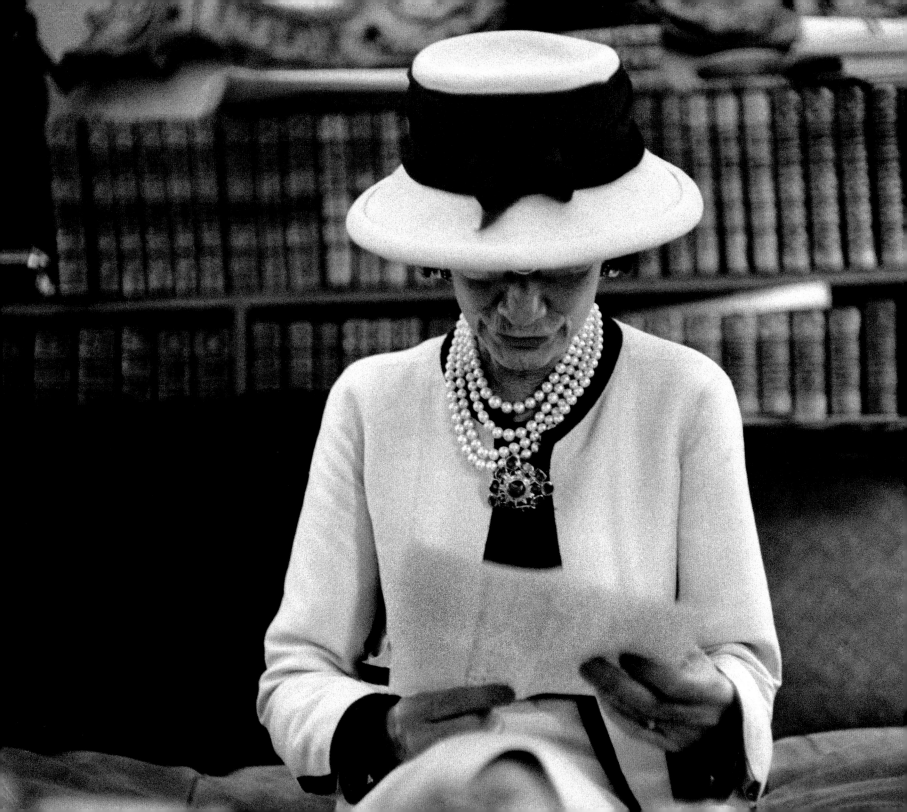

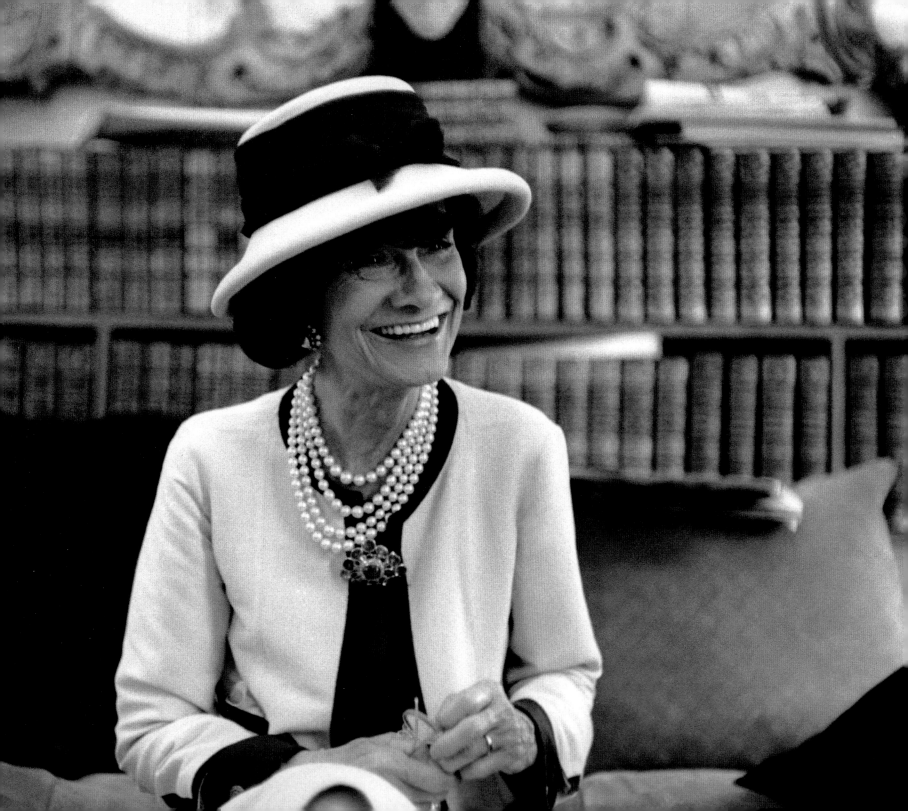

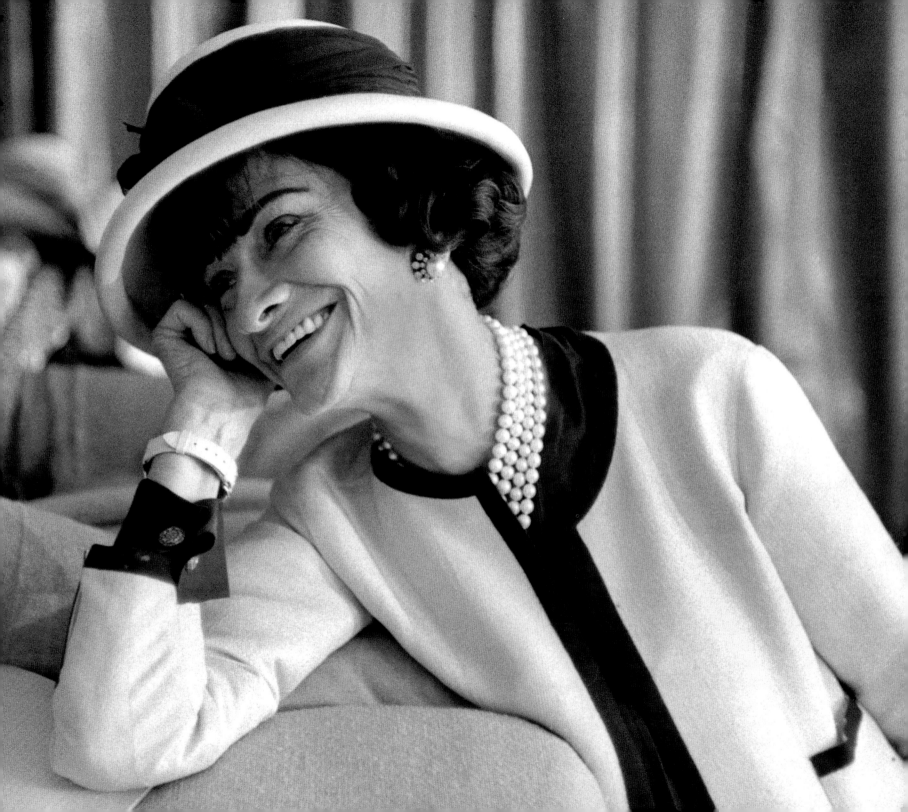

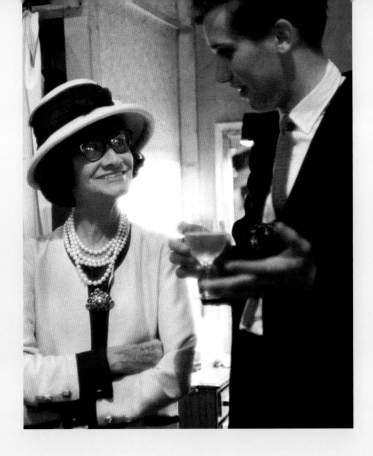

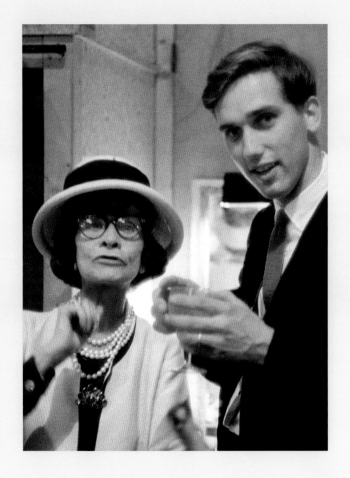

Coco Chanel
and Douglas Kirkland   Summer 62

Edited by Gerhard Steidl

First edition 2009

© 2009 Douglas Kirkland for the images
© 2009 Karl Lagerfeld for the text

© 2009 Glitterati Incorporated, New York
© 2009 Steidl Publishers for this edition

Book design by Karl Lagerfeld and Gerhard Steidl
Scans by Steidl's digital darkroom
Production and printing: Steidl, Göttingen

Steidl
Düstere Str. 4 / 37073 Göttingen / Germany
Phone +49 551-49 60 60 / Fax +49 551-49 60 649
mail@steidl.de
www.steidlville.com / www.steidl.de

ISBN 978-3-86521-865-0
Printed in Germany